FOREVER MY LOVE

The Quiet Little Bestseller That Works Miracles for Dull Marriages.

A VERY PRACTICAL GUIDE FOR TODAY'S MAN.

"I wish I'd had this book 25 years ago."
—Tim LaHaye, Author of
THE ACT OF MARRIAGE

ABOUT THE AUTHOR

MARGARET HARDISTY has written many short stories and plays. She is a musician, an actress, a director of theatrical productions, a popular speaker, and has a radio program heard throughout the nation. Mrs. Hardisty's attorney husband, who has counseled many couples, urged her to write this book.

FOREVER MY LOVE

What Every Man Should Know About His Wife

MARGARET HARDISTY,

FOREWORD BY TIM LAHAYE

Harvest House Publishers
Eugene, Oregon 97402

To my father,
whose gentleness and strength gave me
an invaluable guide in
choosing a mate, and to the woman
who was blessed with his love—
my mother.

Library of Congress Card
Catalog Number: 74-32644
ISBN 0-89081-140-7

ACKNOWLEDGMENTS

The counsel and aid of certain individuals was so invaluable in writing this book that I would like to thank each one personally in print. However, since the helping hands were so numerous, it would be impractical to do so. Thus, I shall have to be content with thanking you collectively and hope the satisfaction of knowing you had a part in this book will be sufficient.

Margaret Hardisty

Introduction

One of the first things a nationally-known man said to me after I interviewed him for this book was, "I get totally nonplussed at times as to what my wife really wants. If you can give men a how-to handbook, I for one, will be eternally grateful."

My husband, who has handled many divorces and reconciliations in his profession as an attorney, said, "Honey, write the book. It's desperately needed."

Several professional marriage counselors urged me on. As one said, "Men have heard a long time from men on what to do with their wives. They need to hear it from a woman's viewpoint."

So the book was born, but not from one woman's ideas alone. It is the result of talking with many women from all walks of life, and with pastors and marriage counselors. It comes from research in numerous books written by psychologists and others. It draws its material from various surveys, including one we personally conducted. If there be any wisdom in it at all, it is from these earthly sources and from the Greater Source who accomplishes what He will in the way He pleases.

Foreword

Who can understand a woman?

Women are beautiful, alluring, exciting, exasperating, and confusing all at the same time! They cry when they are happy, get excited over little expressions of kindness, become angry at masculine thought patterns. Most men don't understand women!

The feminine voice is being heard today as never before, but men aren't listening. Unfortunately, the majority of women libbers are frustrated, angry women who compound their problems by creating masculine resentment.

This voice is different. Margaret Hardisty is a happily married woman who really understands what makes women "tick," and who knows how women need to be treated. And who is better qualified to tell men how a woman thinks and feels than a woman?

After being married for twenty-seven years, and counseling over twenty-five hundred women, I thought I "knew it all." Therefore, when Margaret asked me to write a forward for this book to men, I had a typically masculine reaction—"What can she tell men that they don't already know?" After reading her manuscript, I found out. Margaret explains it quite simply. Not only are women physically and emotionally different from men, they are psychically different—they think differently. That's the reason your wife does the things she does; thinks the way she thinks.

Let's face it—the sexes are different! The man who approaches his wife the way he treats men will strike out in marriage. But a man may enrich his marriage by using the insights he will discover in this book. I gained several new insights about women that I can use in my personal life and in my talks at Family Life Seminars.

Women are responsive creatures by nature. Do you know how to get the best response from your wife? This book will help you.

Tim F. LaHaye
President, Christian Heritage College
Family Life Seminars

Contents

1

Women Are Illogical!

One friend said to me with all the strength of male certainty, "The biggest problem with women is they are totally illogical!" I laughed out loud. It isn't that women are illogical. They're just on a different wavelength. For instance, a wife may pat her husband's stomach affectionately and say, "You need to stay away from desserts for awhile." He shoots back with, "You aren't exactly a candidate for a model yourself."

The husband goes about his daily affairs, the teasing forgotten. But the wife runs to the mirror, inspects herself, drags out the scales for a weigh-in and remembers the pretty woman who smiled at her husband last week when they went for a walk. And hadn't slim Helen (who never gains a pound) said to her at a party recently "I do believe you've gained weight, dear?"

A day or two later, as husband gives her a bear hug and affectionately states, "Wow, what an arm full!" he may be astounded when she "blows up" or begins to cry. To him, her reactions are illogical. To her, they are a natural result of her concern.

To Carry It Further

Husband says	Wife Thinks In Reaction	Wife Wants To Hear
Yea, you look all right.	He's just saying that.	Look all right? I'll say you look all right. R-r-rowr (in the throat)
Not a bad dinner, although the potatoes were a bit salty.	Gripe, gripe. That's all the appreciation I get.	The dinner was great. That asparagus! Mmmm.
New secretary at the office? Oh, yea, she's not bad looking. In fact	He likes her.	Yea, she's okay. But not to my taste.
(Watching TV-Miss America pageant perhaps) Wow! Woo Woo! Not bad!	Stupid.	Not bad, but not my type. You've got them all beat. (If not true in looks, she has them beat in other ways—like being mother to your children.)
I said you look okay. Now, come on.	I look terrible.	Sweetheart, you're beautiful! Let's get out of here so I can show you off.
(To a friend) Yea, my wife and I do all right. I don't know what I'd do without the old gal, when you come right down to it.	He thinks I'm getting old.	(To a friend) My wife is everything to me. I can't imagine life without her.

What do you do all day, anyway?	Despair too deep for thoughts.	Baby, you must be tired. Why don't you take a little rest before dinner. We can wait.
Love you? If I didn't love you, wouldn't I say so?	He doesn't sound like he loves me.	Love you? Darling, I love you more than life itself. You must never doubt that.
(At bedtime) Night.	Sigh.	Goodnight, love.
You ain't no spring chicken, kiddo.	I suppose he thinks he's eternal youth?	You're more beautiful to me now than when we were married.
What did I do?	He should know. He's insensitive.	Honey, I should know what I've done, but I don't. Please tell me so I won't do it again.
Gray hair? Wrinkles? That's the way it goes, kid.	He doesn't understand.	(taking her in arms) Darling, your wrinkles and gray hair are lovely to me. You grow more precious every year (keeping in mind that some of them are there because of you anyway).
New dress, huh? It looks awful!	I look awful.	Honey, that dress doesn't do you justice. Get something that complements your good looks.
You aren't kidding you're getting fat.	He isn't any Jack La Lanne himself.	I like you any way you are, but it would be nice if you lost some weight. You'd be healthier.
Wow! She's some dish!	I suppose he thinks he looks like Paul Newman?	Nothing.

Hey, Ma, hurry up.	The honeymoon is over.	Are you ready, honey?
Where's my book?	His book is more important than I am.	Hon, have you seen my book? I'm looking forward to a cozy evening at home with you while I read.
Go get yourself a new dress.	He thinks I look crummy.	You're so pretty, why don't you get a new dress to match?

See what I mean? The male character of one famous play asks "Why can't a woman . . . be like me?" But, *vive la différence!* The important thing for a man is to enjoy and utilize to his advantage that wonderful difference that is woman.

One of the wonderful strengths of men, in my opinion, is your ability to think big. You tend to make your decisions on practical reasoning and evaluation and react accordingly. Women approach it a bit differently.

Newlywed Bill brought a bouquet of roses home to his wife one day, and she burst out bawling. After he ascertained that she hadn't been stung on the nose by a bee, it dawned on him that this was her way of expressing her happiness. He also was to find out in months to come that his wife could cry when things *weren't* going just right. He found out, too, that when he asked her to do something, her response depended a great deal on how she was feeling at the time.

For practical Bill, his wife's reactions seem silly. He accuses her of putting on an act or of being a prima donna which sends her even further into an emotional display. Eventually, this will cause her to keep her true feelings to herself with a resultant drawing away from marital intimacy.

Chris, on the other hand, handles his wife's outbursts by punishing her. He stays at the office late. Or he won't speak to her for a few days.

Both men fail to understand their ladies and some

day they may find themselves in the same position as Jerry. He's been married for 28 years and is thinking strongly of divorce. His wife hardens her lips when she kisses him. Her voice is hard, too, not like the sweet one he used to hear in happier days. On top of it, he is convinced she is frigid. When he brought her a bouquet of flowers, trying to break through the shell, she just shrugged and went about her housework.

None of these men dream that the reason behind their wives' reactions is themselves.

The Weak One

Your woman is unique. She is different from any other woman created. But there is one basic way in which she is like every other woman created. She, by nature, approaches life from an emotional plane. Whether she reacts coolly or tempestuously, she is an emotional creature, and this is especially true where her relationship with her man is concerned.

She wants to be the "everything" in your life. She wants to be the warmth in your sun, the milk in your gravy, the steel in your bridge. Paradoxically her very nature cries out for someone to lean and depend upon, all the while remaining independent. A woman who shares in a sexual experience with a man considers each moment of love, whether enjoyable or not, a deep part of her life. To a man, such an interlude can be but a moment in time when he is satisfying a physical need. But a woman has to possess that man as her own and to feel that he is so in love with her that this act, no matter how often repeated, is important to him because he is with the one who means everything to him. She needs the certainty that he couldn't bear to have anyone but her. She needs a protector who makes her feel feminine and all woman, precious and cared for. She needs MAN as God intended him to be. If man supplies her need, in every area of her life, it will give him the power necessary to have her practically worshipping at his feet, adoring him and wanting to serve him.

Thus we find the meaning behind the biblical injunction, ". . . husbands, dwell with them according to knowledge, giving honor unto the wife, as unto the weaker vessel." You bet you're the stronger one, for her great weakness is in her emotional needs. The three men mentioned earlier have not understood this, or if they have, they haven't cared. They would rather handle it in what they consider the manly way. No wonder they're having problems.

The Hidden Pearl

History was a drag to me. I love a creative approach to anything, and my history teachers were anything but creative. Their great joy lay in dates, such as 1951 B.C. when what's-his-name was laid to rest in a what-was-it? That was in Turkey, wasn't it, after he fought a war with someone? But at this point in my life, I find it difficult to understand why my teen-age daughter considers history a drag as I did, because I've done an about-face. I love reading about old what's-his-name and why he conquered . . . what's-the-place? And some things I read strike deep into my memory bank. Here's a little historical bit of wisdom I've discovered that you, as a husband, might find most fascinating. I took it from Holy Scriptures, and I am quoting from the Amplified Version. It states that a wife who is doing what she should ". . . respects and reverences her husband—that she notices him, regards him, honors him, prefers him, venerates and esteems him; and that she defers to him, praises him, and loves and admires him exceedingly."

Wow! What a pearl! This isn't a slave we're hearing about. Obviously the legendary wife mentioned here couldn't reverence and admire her husband exceedingly, loving him, if she weren't enjoying it. A woman like that would have to be a contented wife, a very wise person, who would be a friend to her husband and do all she could to fulfill his needs.

Is your mouth watering? Watering or not, admit it or not, I suspect that only an unfeeling scrooge, or a man who has been deceived into thinking that an unhappy state of existence is really a happy one, would fail to admit that he would enjoy a wife like that! Take courage, beleaguered husband. She can be yours! Through using a proper tool—YOU—for opening the oyster, and through applying the POWER that is yours and which is God given, you can have a wife like that. What do you want your wife to be? A better cook? A better mother? A better housekeeper? A better bed partner? It can be yours. Do you wish her to remain young, vibrant and lovely until "death do you part"? There is a way.

You, in all your wonderful masculinity, individuality and personality are being called to battle. You in your manly strength and appeal. You in your handsomeness. You can help your wife become the woman you want her to be. The job may be easy and you'll wonder why you didn't start long before now. The job may be very difficult, but RISK IT! It will pay off and you'll spend the rest of your time together, not putting up with the status quo, contemplating divorce, or looking for greener pastures, but in peace and harmony with the thrill of a newly found, young-again romance thrown in for good measure.

> "When faced with a mountain, I will not quit. I will keep on striving until I climb over, find a pass through, tunnel underneath—or simply stay and turn the mountain into a gold mine—with God's help."
> Robert Schuller
> Hour Of Power, Garden Grove, California

•

P.S. To the wife who is peeking at her husband's book: This may be your opportunity! Whatever happens, be ready to meet him all the way!

2

Men to Arms!

When a man says, "Where did you get this meat?" a
woman replies, "Why, don't you like it?" not because
she is unable to take directness and honesty so much
but because her basic nature wants her man to be
totally satisfied and pleased with everything she does.

An awareness of this truth is your KEY to the
treasures that lie behind a locked door of uncertain
leadership. One man said, "Women just wait to be
supplied so that they may return the favor. Men are
not as willing to give as women, but would do so if
they knew what to give and it didn't take too much
effort." All things which reach a point of excellence
or *arete*, as the ancient Greek puts it, require effort
and time. A man will give unlimited hours and energy

to his work or a hobby because it brings him money, relaxation or pleasure. Does that sound like you? Then are you willing, if necessary, to give unlimited hours and energy to whatever it takes to make your relationship with your wife reach a level of *arete?*

The Spoils Go to the Victor

I am a conquered woman and I exult in it! I adore my conqueror. My life is patterned to please him and to incur even his slight displeasure is a crisis for me. That truth is amazing! Listen, when I was in my early twenties I had made up my mind that marriage was definitely not for me. It wasn't because my childhood was not secure, for my parents were definite in their love for one another. They had a struggle because, just six years after they were married the depression of 1929 hit. Before that shock wave that nearly destroyed our country, they were anything but affluent. In fact, if the social workers and bleeding hearts of today had been operating then, they would have attempted to rush them off to the recipients of a poverty program. Only, they wouldn't have gone. They were proud like many people in those days, and to take financial help from anyone would have been a deep shame. Several years before I was born, the only house they could find had walls with quarter inch cracks between the boards. Mama always said laughingly, "They were so wide, I could throw a cat through them." When the winter wind whistled in, they covered the cracks with heavy building paper. The floor was so cold that if Mother spilled water or milk, it froze the second it touched. They had three children by then, with one tiny baby crawling on that frozen territory.

There was very little fresh food available for there was not enough water for growing vegetables and what they were able to get had to be stored in a cellar for winter use. A plague of grasshoppers wiped out their wheat and for five years they never saw a blade of green grass.

Those were rough times, but they didn't wallow in self-pity. They had a job to do and they did it. My parents never became affluent and aren't today, but what they have they got by themselves, with God's help. They have never needed to feel ashamed. They never took the easy way out.

Yes, times were hard, for long years, and as I saw my dad struggle to pay off medical bills while my sister hid her only shoes with holes in the bottom so Daddy wouldn't feel burdened about them, I began to form opinions about the holy state of matrimony. When I saw my mother, weary to the bone, mopping the floors late at night, my doubts became even deeper. When she received a telephone call to substitute teach, I felt the joy and importance that was hers as the entire family rallied around to help so that Mama could get to school on time to make a little extra money which she proudly saved to buy gifts for Daddy at birthday and Christmas.

Other women influenced my thinking about marriage. One was a friend of the family who sobbed to my mother because she was getting no pleasure at all out of her love life with her husband. Of course, I wasn't supposed to be listening, but that didn't keep me from doing so, and I remember Mama's answer, "Now, dear, that's the way men are." Somehow I instinctively knew that Mother didn't have that same problem, but definite conclusions were forming in my thinking. Women were on earth to serve men! It didn't matter whether they wanted to or not. I *would not*, I decided. Boyfriends found my attitude of "like it or lump it" intriguing. I had my share of marriage proposals, but I wasn't turned from my forming resolve: I would not get married, or if I did, it would be much, much later. I was going to have a piece of that joy and importance that surrounded Mom when she went away to teach and got away from the deadly routine of housework and kids. I would have a career.

I Didn't Understand Myself

Becoming a schoolteacher was only a stepping stone. A world of lights beckoned to me out there and I was responding. What I didn't realize is that basically I needed someone, a close friend, a lover, a relationship that would give a more lasting satisfaction than singing my way through "Finian's Rainbow."

When I met George, I was amazed. The "in" thing at that time among young men was to be cynical, sophisticated and not too interested in anything but making money or getting their names in lights. George came on like a cold drink after a long, hot bicycle ride. He was interested in making money, too, but the teeming joys and surprises of life were more important to him. Our courtship was a whirl of everything from symphonies to canoe trips. So, it should have come as no surprise to find out that he would be different from the average husband. He was a man who saw the oyster and knew there *had* to be a pearl inside there *somewhere*. He instinctively sensed that he, the strong one, would be the tool for opening that oyster, and I, the weak one, would emerge the jewel he wanted me to be, and furthermore, I would love it!

His strategy began on our first date, but the strength of it was put to the test later on.

Time to Grow Up

On a lovely, balmy summer evening in our cozy suburban home, Vesuvius erupted. Methodically, I lifted each piece of silverware from its resting place in the drawer and threw it across the floor with all the tenseness and frustration in each throw that I could muster. My husband walked in just as my throwing spree ended. I burst out, tears adding to my inability to see straight, "You don't care about me! You come home and spend your time in the garden. I need help!" Actually that wasn't what was bothering me. I was weary from having given birth to one baby, caring for him by the hour and being pregnant with another. My frustrations were mounting because the career I had always wanted seemed further away than ever. I was no longer independent and free. I was restricted. I couldn't have my own way. I had to grow up and I didn't know how.

George is not Mr. Milktoast. His personality is a very strong one, and he never hesitates to speak his mind or insist on anything if he feels it is warranted. He could have reacted in several different ways that night, had he chosen:

. . . He could have assumed I was hysterical and slapped me.

. . . He could have lashed me with his tongue.

. . . He could have walked out and not come back until I had cooled down.

Instead he said, "I'm sorry, honey. I should have been in here helping you." The bellows blew empty. I was placated. My respect for him jumped to a new height, for I knew he was not at fault. And so began the long, patient molding of an immature girl into the mature woman that my husband wanted, with all the qualities he desired.

Let's Get Down to Basic Facts

Silly though it may sound to your practical mind, storybook marriages do exist. I know of several and I have one. They are a bit of heaven on earth. But they don't just happen. They are the result of deliberate achievement.

Some of the greatest achievers in business today are the list makers. List making may not be your thing. It isn't mine. But I try to do it anyway, because it is a tremendous organizer and incentive. It clarifies matters when you see them in black and white.

For or against, now is a good time to make a short list, as you evaluate and analyze your situation with your wife. When she isn't around, put down the things you would like to see changed in her. It might go like this:

I want my wife to:

1. Be a better housekeeper
2. Enjoy sexual relations more
3. Be able to take criticism
4. Let me have more to say about the children's discipline
5. Look lovely when I get home
6. Not yell at the kids

If you give in to the temptation of her urgings and let her see your list, your cause may be set back and the ground you lose will be hard to regain. If your wishes are reasonable you can expect to see a majority of them come true if you set out to change your lady in the right way. Don't worry about those that don't start changing immediately. As your wife begins the metamorphosis from caterpillar to butterfly, you will have all you can do to enjoy the nice things that start coming *from her* to you.

Secondly, make a list of the things you *like* in your wife. The story is told of a young woman in pioneer days who was full of spirit. She was strong-willed, joyful, happy and a leader. She married an older man who believed that women should be seen and not heard. She was to work quietly, uncomplainingly, for long hard hours, and then climb into bed at night to fulfill her marital duties. Her very nature cried out against her fate. She wanted to enjoy life. She wanted to make a game out of her work. Her husband determined that hers was a rebellious spirit and he would break it if it took him all his life. He could have taken what he considered her weaknesses, and with wisdom, have turned them into strengths, utilizing them to his advantage, but instead he went about killing the goose that laid the golden egg. He belittled her. He ridiculed her. He criticized her. He held a club over her head and brought it down hard whenever she showed any independence. And then he found, to his sorrow, the very thing that attracted him to her in the first place was gone. She was no longer sparkling and beautiful, but she had given up and lived the rest of her life broken, hurt, tired and old.

Perhaps your protective nature cries out against such a man. He should have been horsewhipped, you might say. The law has cut down on wife beating in our country, but just as bad for a woman is the breaking of her spirit by a man who does not understand or care about her deepest feelings or needs. This man may wake up some morning to realize he no longer likes his wife. She is not attractive to him. She is tiresome and boring and he hasn't the slightest notion that he has been the one who has brought about the unwelcome change.

So our next list might be all the things about your wife that you like and don't want changed.

1. She's a good cook.
2. She stays within her budget.
3. Her counsel is helpful.
4. She doesn't hold a grudge.
5. She has a good sense of humor.
6. She's creative.

This list can be shown to her or fixed up nicely and given to her as a gift on a special day.

You Might Be Surprised

After making the last list, you may decide she isn't so bad after all and make up your mind to keep on putting up with the things you don't like. And you may be listening to your ego, convincing yourself that your wife is *completely* satisfied with the situation as it is. After all, she may even have said so. Would she *dare* say otherwise?

The survey[1] we conducted pointed out that many women have areas in their lives which they would have different if they could. With urging from the liberationists, that sort of thinking could become dangerous.

Jeannie, who has been married 19 years, confided in me, "My husband loves me dearly. I know that. He treats me better than most men treat their wives, but he still is not giving me what I need. I am just not a complete woman." Most people who know her believe that her marriage is ecstastically happy and almost perfect. But it isn't.

Pauline, who has been married nearly 30 years said, "Oh, I've been blessed with a fantastic guy. He's really been wonderful to me." She tells herself this regularly, and she tells her husband. But in a need to unburden her heart, she added wistfully, "It would have been nice if, through the years, he had realized some of my needs and had done something about them. His desires have usually come first."

Another told me, "I'm terribly ashamed of it, and it is horrible to look back on, but I was so desperate for my husband to give me what I needed emotionally, I got involved in a love affair with another man. My husband doesn't know this."

Still another woman, married 25 years, just walked out one day, leaving her husband and three teenagers to shift for themselves. When asked why, she said, "My husband bore down on me for years, not caring about what I thought or felt. I took it as all 'good wives' should, but finally I just couldn't take it any longer." Her husband was so shattered that he did a complete about face, wooed her and won her back to an entirely different married life from the one she had before.

Why do you think the women's freedom movement has made such strides in an amazingly short time? They are striking a responsive chord! And women are listening! They are reevaluating their positions. But you needn't feel angered or frightened over what is taking place. You are merely hearing the heartcry of women whose basic emotional needs are never met by their men! They don't understand it, either, and are searching for the answer in ways that will give them some satisfaction in the absence of the one thing they basically desire.

Jesus told the story of a man who built his house on sand. When the waves came, the sand was washed away and the house fell. It crashed! It was destroyed. Your house may not fall, but it might be imperfectly built, with green boards instead of seasoned ones, with sloppy workmanship instead of that of a skilled master. It may have all the bobbles and mistakes of a carpenter who couldn't care less, as long as he gets his paycheck. If so, your house eventually will begin to get drafty and creaky.

Analyze

One of the most exciting and helpful books on the market, in my opinion, is one my husband keeps on the shelf in his law office for counseling. It is entitled *Spirit Controlled Temperament*, by Tim LaHaye. I had psychology courses in college like everyone else, but here is a book that showed me in my language why I am like I am. It helped me understand my husband better. It helped me realize why my children react as they do. Basically it deals with the four major temperaments that people are born with throughout the world: Sanguine—Mr. Charming Happy-Go-Lucky; Choleric—Mr. Strength and Drive; Melancholy —Mr. Gifted Perfectionist; Phlegmatic—Mr. Slow and Lovable. In analyzing your wife's uniqueness, it would be a tremendous help for you to get a copy of that book. You will see why she doesn't look at things the way you do (aside from her being female) and why you were attracted to her in the first place. You'll also be better equipped to deal wisely with your wife's weaknesses as you start to bring out the beauty that lies dormant within her.

Keep in mind, however, that underlying all the temperaments women are basically the same emotionally—each must have her emotional needs as a woman met if she is going to respond in the way every man longs to have his woman respond.

The minister who married George and me wrote in the back of our "Marriage Service" booklet:

> "Love is that which causes one person to desire the most good to come to another *and* is willing to do whatever is necessary to bring it about."
>
> Rev. G. W. Blount

At that time I little appreciated the concern of that dear elderly man, but now I know what he was trying to tell us.

•

P.S. to the fascinating woman still peeking at her husband's book: When you come to think of it, we women do have some weaknesses, don't we? Never mind about *his*. His will begin to change as he tries to help you. And his change will come much faster if you meet him more than halfway. Go to work on those sluggish areas now and begin to reap the benefits.

3

Good Grief, Woman, What Do You Want?

If your woman is like most, the important thing is not whether you are rich or poor or whether you have furnished her with a hut or a palace. She isn't overly concerned about whether you are suave or rough, sophisticated or ordinary. She isn't interested that much in whether you are tall or short. All she wants is for you to treat her the way she longs to be treated. Only when that is missing does she wish fervently for something else and begins to think, "If only . . . ."

I suppose most men are aware that their wives' eyes light up at the thought of going out to dinner and realize they are pleased when they bring them gifts. And many men would be willing to do anything to keep that light shining in their wives' eyes if they knew how to go about doing it. It's amazingly simple to do.

Romance Me, Please

At the top of most women's list when it comes to what they want from their husbands is ROMANCE. This truth was borne out very clearly in our survey and in personal interviews. But your wife's idea of romance and your idea of what it means, may be two different things. Romance in the male mind is what he does in order to get his wife in the right frame of mind for sex. That isn't the way a woman thinks at all. But whether or not she is able to respond *fully* to you in your physical relationship will depend largely on whether or not you supply her with *her* idea of romance.

A very popular and beautiful actress was being interviewed on radio following the publication of her book containing beauty secrets. The interviewer, a man, spent little of the time discussing the book. He seemed most interested in the fact that she had just divorced her producer husband. They batted the reasons for the divorce back and forth at length, especially since she stated that she and her ex-husband were still very much in love but that they just couldn't live together anymore. The interviewer seemed to have decided in his own mind that the reason had to be because she had a career outside the home which just didn't mix with her husband's career. I listened with great interest, for I felt, if she were a typical woman, no matter how career minded she was, the career was not the problem. Sure enough, after a time, the real causes came out. Rather wistfully she commented that in 19 years of marriage, they had never sat through a meal together without the phone ringing for him and he taking the call. She said she felt as if she were an extension of his business. She went on to confide that they didn't talk about intimate things. She told about the "little things" that disturbed her. Since he felt it unnecessary to correct them, the "logical" thing in their minds was to get a divorce. Here was a woman who had a world idolizing her, but all she really wanted was romance from her husband.

Words, Words, Words

"Pleasant words are like an honeycomb, sweet to the soul, and health to the bones," the proverb states. Remember the husband-wife conversations in Chapter 1? *How* you say it is important! It doesn't take much to adjust your communication so that you set your wife glowing instead of resenting. Once you practice awhile and get the hang of it, you'll find it rather fun, for the results you see will astound you. You may be saying, "I can't watch my every word." That's what teen-agers will say about their inability to stop cursing, but I notice they are able to watch every word very carefully indeed if there is someone present they want to impress with how nice they are. Theirs is a cop out. Yours may be laziness.

Sweet Nothings

Words like "Poopsy" and "Babykins" may not be to your liking, but most people can adjust to "Sweetheart," "Honey" and "Darling." Some husbands are willing to supply a few of those at bedtime, but in daytime can show an amazing lack of skill in handling women.

A man who is going to outsmart his wife will be liberal in his use of them. You may be laughing at the absurd picture of you whispering sweet nothings in a practical situation, and you may be saying, "My wife would think I was nuts." But it's like anything in life. If you do it with quiet confidence, and you are totally serious, it won't take her long to realize that you aren't poking fun at her and that you really are trying to say something. The first few days or even weeks she may do a double take or even tell you to quit that nonsense, but inside, she'll be glowing and probably will begin to accept it openly in time, with sweetness and love.

It can backfire, of course. One young husband I know hesitates to ever say anything complimentary because his wife, in her eagerness to let him know this is what she really wants, overdoes her response and practically attacks him. He finds her display a bit much. It should be a signal to him, however, that she's crying for more attention. If he would supply it, she would calm down.

Do You Love Me?

Our survey pointed out very emphatically that men find it important to be told by their wives that they love them, with many of them voting for an everyday experience. How much more so does a woman require those three words! Words are important to a woman. Several men have said to me, "If I told my wife I loved her every day, the words would become cheap." We were interested in finding through our survey that the men who supplied lots of romance to their wives, generally stayed true to form in telling their wives daily and sometimes several times a day that they loved them. And if that doesn't impress you, maybe this will: those proved to be the most stable and well rounded marriages with the happiest wives. Words never become cheap to a woman if they are said sincerely. Some women don't react visibly to outward displays of affection from their husbands, but you can be sure they are reacting underneath the surface . . . and favorably.

The old saw, "She knows I love her," is not enough. Showing your love by working hard and providing her with material goods is not enough. Many a woman would trade her beautiful home for a hut where love and romance are synonymous. One woman did just that. Her husband, enormously successful financially, was so busy proving his love for his wife by expanding his empire but failing to supply the romance she craved, that he was amazed when she ran off with one of his hired hands—a dashing, handsome, romantic Mexican. She forfeited her fortune just to find the real things a woman desires.

Remember, you are the man who at one time, was the prince of your wife's dreams. You were her knight on a white charger whom she married to carry her off to a land where love never dies and romance goes on and on. You were the most intelligent, most handsome and most clever man in the world and she let everybody know it. A wife may take a year, or perhaps two before she is willing to admit that her hero isn't a hero after all. He's a stubborn, unfeeling character who refuses to tell her he loves her every day. Since this is one of her greatest needs, she often feels when he does say it, he doesn't really mean it, or he would make sure she heard it all the time! And that's some feminine logic, or lack of it if you wish, that puts it straight.

With all the romance and sweetness my husband brought into my life from the beginning of our marriage, he didn't tell me he loved me but occasionally. I knew he loved me. I knew he adored me. But I wanted to hear those words more often. It took years for me to convince him of that, but now he supplies that need generously, whispering it to me when I'm in his arms at night, laughing it to me while we're running and playing with the children, grabbing me while I'm doing a chore to hold me briefly while he tells me, mouthing it to me when we are in a crowd. How secure it makes me feel! How it causes my doubts to flee.

"I consider that ridiculous," you may be saying. But if you knew you could start a glow within your wife that would, if the treatment continued, shine brighter and brighter until it began to manifest itself in utter heartfelt devotion to you, wouldn't it be worth it?

If you really *don't* love your wife anymore, but you would like to keep the marriage together, you can always find something you *can* "love" every day. Her cooking, if nothing else. Perhaps you can tell her sincerely that you love her hair or her lips, and soon you may be saying "I love you" to her once again and meaning it. She may start falling in love with you again, too, for love begets love.

Get Started

So use your man-mind to look beyond the momentary discomfort you feel at even attempting something you dislike doing and get started on your strategy. So far we have found that you must...

1. Determine not to settle for the status quo.
2. Decide what changes you would like to see in your wife.
3. Analyze her basic temperament.
4. Watch your language; choose your phrases carefully so they are music to her ears.
5. Bathe her in endearing terms.
6. Unleash a stubborn tongue so it can say "I love you" to her several times a day.

You've got a good start and an important one. But if you really want to be the man among men, you'll want to consider other ways of romancing your wife. A man who would have a wife who adores him will get in the habit of touching her hair as he goes by (gently, friend), taking her hand and kissing it occasionally (no, not mockingly), helping her with her chair at dinner (yes, even at home) and helping her on with her coat. He will open doors for her (insisting that she wait in the car until he has time to get around), not allow her to carry heavy loads, wink at her across the room, inquire if she is warm enough and ad infinitum. It's so easy to be thoughtful once you set your mind to it. The amazing thing about this kind of gentlemanly conduct is that you will find yourself carrying it over into other parts of your life, and as a bonus you will begin to enjoy the "adoration" of other women as well.

One Norwegian beauty made a public statement to the effect that American men are the most charming in the world. They worship women according to her. They are so polite. If you were such a celebrity's husband, would she think the same of you?

But as you charm other women, keep in mind (in case your head begins to turn and you start getting ideas) that the most appealing man in the world is the one who treats every woman he meets as if she were something special, doing the gentlemanly things for her, but *remaining unavailable*. His wife always comes first. And there's power in that sort of strength, Sir.

Say It Another Way—With a Gift

I find it absolutely astounding that there are people who never receive gifts from their mates, even on birthdays and Christmas! Lack of money is no excuse. A gift can be a handmade card or a dime store item. If you can afford expensive gifts your wife will love them, but the little things are important to her, too.

Although I have had my share of lovely flower arrangements from the florist, especially planned ones with forget-me-nots arranged with carnations or roses, on unspecial days I have been just as pleased when my husband comes in holding a bunch of flowers he has picked up at the supermarket for a dollar. And I hold very tenderly in my heart the many times he has stopped working long enough in the yard to enter the house, dirty and sweaty, to hand me a tiny rose bud or the first crocus of spring.

Our survey showed that most women preferred romantic or frivolous gifts to expensive or practical ones. The men generally admitted that they gave practical ones or ones that had sexual overtones. Of course, she needs a toaster, but . . . let me ask you something. When you need a hammer, do you wait until Christmas to get one? I doubt it. You probably pick it up at the hardware store on the way home. Why, then, should your wife have to wait for the special days for her "tools"? Those can be your un-special day gifts. They can surprise her when she least expects it. But gifts for special days—Christmas, birthdays, and anniversaries—should be something lovely—like a music box, a ring, a beautiful vase, an outfit she's wanted but felt she couldn't afford or a very special piece of jewelry. Nightgowns and perfumes should be only occasional or when she specifically requests them.

Don't forget other "special days." Valentine's Day can bring a lovely little apron and hanky (not candy for most women are on diets), and Easter can be a wonderful time for a white rose to plant in the garden just for her, to "remind you every year that I love you more."

It is different for men, of course. You might *prefer* a shovel to a new shirt. A typical reaction (to my consternation) on what to get my husband for a special day was what I heard on our last anniversary. He responded, "That's easy. I need a sledgehammer handle." And that's no joke. A sledgehammer handle! Many times through the years I longed to get him something "romantic" like some jeweled cuff links, or a ruby dinner ring, and I have been absolutely in heaven when his watch no longer runs and I can buy him a new one, but I have deferred to the fact that he much preferred a wrench set or a saw on most occasions. Because I love him and want to please him, I will continue to buy the things that he desires if I am able. Conversely he has been wise enough to do the same for me, and each "lovely" I have in the house reminds me over and over again that he cared about my desires.

Of course, it is vitally important that you pick out any gift to give her, yourself. One lawyer's wife I know received a gift from her husband for her birthday that was picked out by his secretary. He had been extremely busy in trial all week and just couldn't seem to get to the store. It was a lovely, expensive gift, but it went crashing into the wastepaper basket when she found out who shopped for it. Many women wouldn't have the nerve to do that, but would ache inside the rest of their lives with a very special hurt.

•

P.S. Whoops, there lady! Be careful you don't take advantage! As he ventures into this new approach with you, gently remind him that you have no desire to ruin his budget. And I know that you know, only a wretch would make fun of her lover's attempts at romance, which could be a bit clumsy at first. Respond in a big way, okay? Let him know you like it.

4

Let's Continue

Perhaps you are on a very tight budget and eating out seems out of the question. It reminds me of a friend of ours who is now a college president. When he was going through seminary, he and his wife were living a real hand-to-mouth existence. Their apartment was tiny and poorly furnished, but they had a happy marriage because he realized, even at that young age, the importance of romance. They would save a few pennies every time he had the opportunity to preach at a local church where he received a few dollars as an honorarium. Gradually, their fund built up and with a feeling of great festivity, they would dress in their shabby best, hunt up the least expensive restaurant they could find, order a steak dinner and divide it in half as they enjoyed each other and their love. Those days have brought them many wonderful memories as they remember their hilarious laughter around the lone candle that burned on the restaurant table.

She'll Know You Care

There are other ways, too, if you really care about your wife's needs. You can always telephone ahead, saying, "Don't cook, hon. Just get the candles on the table. I'm bringing home a little surprise." And you show up with something from the delicatessen, or a take-out place. To make it really special, you might run to the supermarket and get an inexpensive bunch of flowers which are just as pretty as those from the florist's (which can be reserved for the super special days when you get that raise or a windfall from other quarters). Or you can pick a fistful of flowering weeds from the roadside if nothing else. The important thing is, you are showing her that you are thinking of her in a special way and want to make her happy.

The absolutely necessary once-a-week dinner out idea seems a bit much in these days of high cost. But women insist on it because it is the one way they can force some romance into their lives when it is lacking in other ways. You'll find, when you start supplying in the other ways, you won't have to take her out so often. She won't feel the need. But when you do take her out, make it a festive occasion.

The experience of one friend isn't unusual. She says, "When my husband does ask me out to dinner, which is seldom, I get all excited. But when we get there, he is so unresponsive and seems so concerned about the cost, that the romance I had anticipated is gone. I'm just sitting in a restaurant instead of on the cloud I had envisioned, wondering how many other couples there find each other so uninteresting that they have nothing fascinating to talk about." A woman wants to believe you are taking her out because you want to be alone with her in a romantic spot. She wants to believe you feel she is worth every penny of it. If you are prepared mentally with several interesting topics to discuss, you will find it fun, too.

Keep in mind that a dinner at McDonald's or the nearest "all you can eat for $2.50" place is all right when you take the children along, but when it's just the two of you, it is worth going less often and taking her to a top spot where you can relax for an hour or two with all the fixings.

Going out to eat was never one of my hangups, probably due to the fact that I have enough of it with my concerts and speaking engagements. Another reason, undoubtedly, has been the way my husband has complimented my cooking so profusely. He really has me convinced that he thinks I'm the best cook in the world, so I enjoy preparing meals for him. I even enjoy my own cooking, thanks to him. There was a time when I felt a need to go out to eat more often. My husband, who by now was sure he couldn't digest anyone's food but mine, didn't want to bother, and it became a polite clashing of the wills. At least, I started telling myself, he could invite me out on Mother's Day, or after church so I could rest on Sunday. But he had made up his mind, and generally when my husband makes up his mind, I pursue the subject no longer for it is useless. However, typical of his desire to have an ideal marriage, he did rally, and it happened quite by accident. His brother and wife were visiting and somehow the subject opened up on all the lovely restaurants they like to eat in since they go out at least once a week. I made the comment that I wished we could go out more than twice a year, and my husband came back with, "But we aren't going to." Then I said, "It's all right. When I feel the need to go out, I just call a friend and we have lunch together. I provide my own romance." He picked up the distress signal, set his own desires aside, and made an appointment to take me to lunch every week from then on. As it was, the luncheon engagements weren't filled because we were both too busy to keep them. But the few we were able to indulge in were marvelously memorable. I was convinced that he would do anything to make me happy and as soon as I knew that, I didn't feel neglected any longer.

She Needs to Get Away

Plan a weekend away without the children occasionally. Pick the nicest hotel you can afford, let her buy something new for the occasion and go away determined to give her all your attention. Tell her constantly how lovely she is and how happy you are to be married to her. Use that weekend to make her feel very loved.

She's More Important Than Other People

Some men have a tendency to think there are areas which are sacred to their manhood and should not be polluted by their wives' intrusion. Their women would never dare call their husbands at the office. A woman who does so finds her husband's voice cool. In fact, he may act so impatient and put out that it ruins the whole day for her. Naturally there are certain occupations where such an occurrence, except in an emergency, would result in his being fired. But a man who has an independent office should keep in mind that, even though his work is very important, hers is, too. He wouldn't hesitate to call *her* if he wanted something done, or needed to share something. She would be expected to not only receive his calls with politeness, but with warmth as well. She deserves to be treated with the same courtesy by him.

George calls me quite often, and though I'm sometimes right in the middle of a song I'm composing or a story I'm writing, I'm always delighted to hear his voice. He acts the same with me. If he's in a conference that can't be interrupted, he usually says, "I'll call you back as soon as I'm through, dear." Generally, he takes the call anyway because he knows my time is tight and when I call, it's for a good reason. In all our years of marriage he has never made me feel like I am bothering him and that he isn't pleased I called. If you let your secretary or nurse or others know that your wife's calls are priority, they won't resent her calling either and make her feel like an intruder when they answer the phone. Remember, she's the most important woman in the world to you, or should be, and you shouldn't care what anybody thinks.

Hey, Over There

When you are with other people, make it a special point to single her out a few times during the evening. A wink or a soft look across the room, a quick hug as you say something to her, holding her hand if you are sitting beside her, making sure you don't pay more attention to the other attractive women at the gathering than you pay her will do wonders to keep her assured of your love.

If You Travel

Many marriages have failed unnecessarily because the husband is away a lot. One evangelist, who travels all over the world, is a classic example of what can be done in successfully handling a wife and six children. He calls at least once a week to speak to the children's problems and to advise them concerning his ideas, whether he's in San Francisco or Africa. Even though he is on a fixed, modest salary the cost is well worth keeping in touch with the situation at home. How often the expansive salesman blusters in the front door and goes about the business of setting things in order after he's been away for a week or two. How often this same man finds his children rebelling when they are old enough to do so. This man has a double responsibility. While he's away, if he is wise, he will woo his wife . . . and his children. He'll send little gifts, write letters (separate ones occasionally for each of the younger children) and keep his fingers in the decision making by calling frequently. He'll send an "I love you" telegram or wire some flowers. Your wife may already harbor doubts about what you are doing while she stays at home with the children. And you are well aware of the temptations constantly thrown your way, including your own needs and desires. Your wife needs to be assured daily, if possible, that you aren't enjoying yourself too much without her.

One man who refused to try to keep family communications going while he was away said, "Look, I called her to let her know where I was staying and told her I loved her at the same time. That was enough." Sometimes he was away for over a week at a stretch. Even though his wife adjusted to the crumbs sent her way over the 23 years of their marriage, she soon lost interest in keeping herself up. His inability to be a complete husband resulted in an incomplete wife so that he lost interest in her and fell in love with another woman who knew her worth and bloomed herself into his life.

Use Your Imagination

Even if you are unimaginative by nature, you can always use ideas you've heard about. One pastor leaves little notes in drawers and cupboards for his wife which contain goodies such as, "There's a rumor going around the church that I'm in love with you." Does her heart sing? You can count on it.

Another exciting way to supply her romance, and

something she'll be sharing with every friend who calls her for the next year or several years is serving her breakfast in bed. You get up early, before she's awake, on a Saturday or Sunday. Call her in time so she can pretty herself up, with instructions that she can't come out of the bedroom because you have a surprise for her. Plan a simple but colorful breakfast, served on a tray with a flower tucked in the corner and a little note which might say, "To the loveliest wife in the world," or "I love you." If your children are allowed to help, no matter how tiny they are, and their spills and mistakes are not berated, they'll get the idea that Mom is pretty special. They'll also understand that it's nice to do special things for others.

I know of one man who sprinkled velvety rose petals all over the bed on his wedding night. Now, that's romance! Why not try it on one of your anniversaries?

Think up some of your own—write a song for her, or a poem. All sorts of ideas will flow if you'll let them.

Very often it's the woman who is told, "Dress as sexy as possible; keep your hair exquisitely groomed; have the house blooming and the food aromatic when he arrives." She's urged over and over again to keep the romance alive in her marriage so her man won't go running off to another woman. Although I agree that women should be doing these things, I feel the emphasis is on the wrong person. A woman *will* do these things, if the husband takes his first responsibility as the KEY to a happy marriage. Instead of having a woman who is desperately trying to hang on to him, he will have one who is beautiful and alluring in her knowledge that he is the cohesive and dependable force that will keep the marriage alive and vibrant.

It Takes Two

One young wife spent the first five years of her marriage trying to get that point across to her husband, but somehow the message just didn't come through. She pointed out romantic things other husbands were doing for their wives, and finally started dressing as alluringly as she could for him, buying the flowers, arranging the candlelight dinners at home and generally breaking her neck to please him. He enjoyed the attention, but his refusal to be romantic for her sake continued. The glow is starting to go out of their marriage now and I wouldn't be surprised if his lovely, breathless young wife will eventually become hard and embittered, finding sex an unwelcome chore.

Darling, I Am Growing Old

As your wife advances in age, she may need romance more than ever. Although a man's horizons tend to broaden as age creeps up, a woman's doesn't. As one friend told me, "You don't think much about it until one day the bag-boy at the grocery store calls you "M'am." Wrinkles, gray hair, figure sagging, seeing younger women looking at her husband in admiration can be a frightening nightmare to the middle-aged and older woman. Every ten years she becomes painfully aware that there is a whole new group of men that no longer find her attractive.

What if your wife were to die or be killed today? Think about it seriously. Even if you haven't been very pleased with her, have no doubt about it, you would feel a deep sense of loss. You would find to your dismay that the washing and ironing wasn't done. There would be no meals on the table when you got up or came home. You would have no one with whom to share your intimate joys and sorrows. You would have to be both father and mother to your children and there would be the realization that nothing would ever be the same again without her.

Now project your thoughts ahead a year or two. Like most widowed men, you would probably come to the conclusion that you needed another wife. You find that it may be cheaper to live alone, but it isn't nearly as interesting. So you meet another woman. You think of her as a possibility for remarriage. What do you begin to do? Of course. You bathe before you go to see her. You put on your flashiest clothes and might even run down to see what's "mod" these days and buy some new outfits. Suddenly you have energy you had forgotten you had for boating, bicycling and golfing. You enjoy taking her to dinner in the loveliest places, holding her hand, having her sit next to you and kissing her goodnight. You feel young again. You may even fall in love again.

This same stimulation, this same feeling of youth, this same excitement can be yours with the woman you chose in the first place, plus the comfortable knowledge that a deep, deep love is there as well. It's all a matter of setting your mind in the right direction and acting on it.

If your wife should outlive you, would she, after the first period of mourning, feel relief that she at last was free? If she remarried, is there a chance that she would be far more "in love" with the second man than with you, because you never met her needs? It has happened. One physically beautiful woman became like a lovely painting on a wall to her husband, seldom noticed or cared for. Her husband was selfish and careless. But her second marriage, after his death, was different. This man appreciated her. He treated her the way she had always dreamed and which was her right. She had loved the first husband but was not sorry he was gone.

Once when I was in high school, my Dad was singing, "Darling, I Am Growing Old," in his lovely tenor voice while I accompanied him on the piano. In the middle of the song his voice broke. Spinning around he walked rapidly to the couch and lay down, his hand shielding his eyes. I rushed heartbroken to my room. Without a doubt, our time here on earth is at best a single note of time in the vast symphony of eternity. Shouldn't we strive, with all our being, not only to prepare for eternal life, but to spend our time bringing as much joy to those we love or should love as we possibly can? What a challenge! What a test of strength! Talk about being all man! The real test has yet to be met by many a male.

*

P.S. Lovely wife, it sounds exciting, doesn't it? I mean, just the thought that he might start doing some of those things! Don't start feeling sorry for yourself if it doesn't happen right away, though. He's thinking about it. Give him time. It's not easy to change habits overnight. You can give him a little boost by preparing romantic situations yourself. You know, candlelight and flowers at dinner or little parties for Valentine's Day or his birthday. Oh, and don't forget the lovely outfit you are going to wear to go along with it—a provocative skirt and blouse or an elegant long gown, just for him.

5

He Turns Me Off

I received a leading Christian magazine for young people and was amazed at the frankness with which the articles discussed sexual relations and its problems. That could be good or bad, depending on your viewpoint. The truth is, we parents cannot guide our young people through the maze of confusion in this field if we are not enjoying success in it ourselves.

One pastor-counselor with whom I discussed this subject estimates that 95% of the marital problems that have come to him in over fifty years of counseling have had a poor sex life as their basis. Generally, the woman, not enjoying it, is resisting and the husband, who wants to enjoy it, resents her resistance. Since sexual pleasure is probably one of the main reasons you married in the first place, and since it is

37

a vitally important aspect of married life, I would like to discuss it frankly from the viewpoint of a woman who has been totally and completely satisfied by a very wise husband since the first day of our honeymoon, and from the viewpoints of many women who have shared with me their thoughts on the matter.

Puritan ethics have been a scapegoat for so long that the usual reason for sexual maladjustment is usually overlooked. It is a widespread problem not limited to people with religious upbringing. Never have the stimuli been so blatant and obvious. Never have so many people been doing it more and enjoying it less. I was in a dress shop one day when I heard blaring over the radio an astounding result of a survey which the announcer said indicated that 80% of the women in the United States had never experienced a climax in the act of sexual intercourse. That included single women as well as married. It was an interesting contrast to a survey taken of American middle-aged women in the 1950s in which it is stated that 67% of the women polled enjoyed a climax "usually or always."[2]

If there is such a thing as a frigid woman, I have yet to meet one. "Ha ha," laughs the husband of a frigid woman. But hear me out. All other things being normal, a woman who dislikes sex and "turns off" is generally a woman who has not been handled correctly.

Francine and Mike were a very attractive young couple with four children. She didn't like him to do anything more than cuddle her in bed, a fact which he complained about long and loud to anyone who would listen. He told me she was frigid. Later, after they were divorced, she came to me after a concert I had given. Since I am always sky-high emotionally and ravenously hungry after my concerts, I invited her to join me in a nearby restaurant to renew our acquaintance. She shared her hopes that Mike would come back someday, but that meanwhile, she was dating again. I recall her gentleness as she said, "After being called an iceberg for so many years and beginning to wonder if it were true, it's a relief to find that I respond very warmly to the men I am dating." Although she was not indulging in premarital sex, because of her religious beliefs, she did marry again, and very happily. Mike simply did not understand the problem and rather than seek a solution for her sake, he stewed in his own juice until his goose was cooked.

The Answer Is You

Dear husband, statistics show once again that the key is strong, exciting swashbuckling YOU. And if you don't fit that picture at this point, you CAN. Unless your wife is physically incapable of normal relations, mentally ill, or severely emotionally handicapped, she can enjoy the sexual act as much as you do, and it is not to your credit if she doesn't.

You may think the ABC's of lovemaking begin in the bedroom. They do not. They began YESTERDAY when your wife first saw you in the early morning. And if you didn't start yesterday, at least you can start TODAY. Before you can turn your wife on, you have to take a good look at the things that turn her off. See if you identify with some of the lovers listed below and try to see them from their wives' viewpoint.

SLOPPY SAM loves to see his wife look "cute." He expects to be greeted at the door each night with a smile, a curly hairdo, ruffles, bows and delightful chatter. While she hovers around him, smacking and hugging, he likes to slip off his tie, shrug out of his coat, peel off his shirt, kick off his shoes and change into a baggy pair of old pants. His well-groomed, sweet smelling, cute little wife sits across the dinner table from this apparition in an undershirt, who hasn't bothered to shower. She puts up with his yawns which he doesn't think necessary to hide. He eats with his mouth open and talks with his mouth full. She chatters on through his burps and says nothing about his elbows which hold him up at the table.

She tries not to notice the difference between the heart-throb on the TV screen and the paunchy belly and crooked spine melted into the cracks of the couch across the room from her. He bellows for his beer, and the cute little trick leaps up to comply. "If she doesn't like it, she can lump it!" he answers indignantly to the deodorant commercial on the boob-tube. Well, despite her pasted on smiles, she doesn't like it, and she isn't lumping it. For Cutie makes him pay for his grossness by her inability to respond to him when he manages to groan his way into bed.

You may say, "My wife doesn't fix herself up like Cutie." You may even have felt the sting of coming home to a wife in her dirty bathrobe and slippers. Her hair may or may not have been combed. Perhaps it was already up in curlers so she would look nice the next day when she goes shopping. Unfortunately, she wasn't able to get up in time to comb it out in the morning so you left for work with your last sight being something ghastly which faintly resembled the woman you married.

Although the majority of men can put up with a messy wife in the morning, it is pretty tough to face the same problem in the evening. Our survey showed that most men would like to have their wives greet them at the door each evening freshly bathed and perfumed, wearing something provocative, hair fixed beautifully and generally making them glad they aren't still at the office with the secretaries. Most of the women admitted on their surveys that they fail in this area. But if you really want your wife to do differently, one of the best ways is to set the example. She will get very nervous after awhile when she sees how terrific you look and realizes how she compares. She'll begin to see you in a new light and want to please you.

A young boy came to visit with us once. All week, he wore his "grubbies." We were going to take him to visit some rather important people, so we wanted him to dress nicely. He became quite angry, saying that his good clothes were for the ride home on the plane and he wasn't going to wear them sooner. How often have you kept your "good clothes" to please the crowd that couldn't care less when you go shopping or to a movie?

If you don't want to turn your wife off, and you want her to be whistle material, when you get home put on an attractive matching sports outfit for her eyes alone. Comb your hair. Brush your teeth. Be appealing.

CRITICAL CURTIS drives up to the house, still frowning over the ridiculous driving of motorists he has passed on the highway, growls at a tricycle that is out of place and mutters under his breath at the finger-marks around the doorknob. He opens the door, steps inside and what should meet his suffering eyes? His wife is on the phone talking with her mother! She doesn't leap to attend to him and his irritation strikes deeper. His little children come rushing down the hall to greet him and step on his shoes, smudging the shine. The house is neat and clean but his wife, in her rush, forgot to put a dustcloth away. He lets her know it. She, off the phone by now, is nervously getting the food on the table. Curtis sniffs the main dish, frowns and says, "I hope the meat isn't gristly." He hangs his clothes neatly in his closet, angrily straightens the bedcover that hangs a little low on one side and goes in to dinner. He is irritated even more because the children want to chatter nonsense at him when he is trying his best to relate to his wife the disgusting ways of certain people he knows at work. All evening he picks at this, pecks at that, critical and disapproving, not noticing all the things that have been prepared for his comfort, or at least not commenting on them. His wife is learning to dislike her husband and her relief is obvious when he leaves every morning. At night, she resents his stilted lovemaking but is too afraid to say anything because, regardless of the circumstances, Curtis is always right. Curtis is not fun to live with.

If you are like Curtis, and wish to change, it might be well to count your daily blessings and dwell on them. Close your eyes to the negative things. Ignore the minor details. Start thinking in terms of the positive and look for something to compliment in every situation, whether at home or at work. Avoid scathing denunciations of anyone, no matter what they've done to you. Your wife may even have joined in with you in this type of reaction to life, becoming like you, but a negative atmosphere does not make for a happy love life.

VOLCANO VICTOR is not unlike Curtis, except that he isn't as well controlled in his disapproval. His family can pretty well predict what kind of evening it's going to be as soon as Papa walks in the door. He's king and they had better well know it. If he's in a good mood, they can have some hilarious moments, for he can be so charming. But Victor is easily offended and should someone say the wrong thing at the wrong time, the volcano erupts! Victor has a right to blow up anytime he well pleases, doesn't he? Isn't he the head of the family? And once he blows, it is very difficult for Victor to change his attitude. His wife has learned it is better to speak softly, step lightly and weigh her words carefully. Victor, used to being selfish, takes his love as he takes everything else—with Victor in mind.

If your volcano erupts too often, or you are easily hurt and offended, you might consider the two-year-old who throws a tantrum when he doesn't get his way. Or the boy at the game who takes his ball and goes home if the kids won't play the way he likes. It's pretty difficult for young people to look up to and admire such immaturity. Cap your volcano and become a strong person.

CRUDE COREY is a man's man. To him, being masculine is proved by how much cursing a man does in his conversation, and how much he can drink without getting stewed. He spits hard and bellows loud. When he walks in the door, he hunts up his wife, pats her on the behind, kisses her wetly and starts to poke at her intimate parts. Throughout the evening, he leers, pinches and feels her. She tells him she doesn't like it, which throws him into guffaws and next time she comes near he continues his barrage of repulsive advances.

One woman of 35, who has become embittered over this very thing, said to me, "I tell him it turns me off, and then he can't understand why I can't respond to him sexually." She's grown old before her time and looks 50 rather than her age.

To women, and to many men, cursing proves not that you are manly but that you have a weak vocabulary. A REAL man NEVER has to prove it. Drinking never yet gave a man charm or masculinity. Instead he gets bad breath, bloodshot eyes and blurred judgment. Smoking is closely correlated.

A man tends to become what he reads, listens to and dwells on. Fill the soul with filth and it becomes a cesspool which begins to affect all of your life, whether you know it or not. Fill the soul with beauty and cleanliness and your relationship with your family will show it. A man who believes the LIE told by the pornographers will never be a good lover, for the very *sensitivity* his wife's emotions demand becomes hardened and self-centered, making common and crude what should be beautiful.

If it is your wife who is crude, consider that anyone can be sucked into a lie. That these things are sophisticated because "the beautiful people" do them proves only that the beautiful people have believed the lie, too. Most women would give these things up (unless its a habit they're hooked on) if they were brought to the point of adoring their husbands and thus wanting to please them.

One lovely young woman, a bride of a year, came to visit us for a week one time. I was delighted to hear her speak about her marvelous husband. She would "follow him to the ends of the earth." She was in love from the top of her head to the tips of her toes. Three years later, they both came to visit with their little children. She was smoking and swearing and he was griping at her. The entire visit was one of quarreling over her habits which he was trying to get her to break. The habits weren't the basic problem, of course, but their incompatibility erupted in this manner. So her habits are not first on your list of redoing your lady, are they? That comes later.

I'll never forget when I was 16, I dated a nice boy from our high school. That evening I used a very crude word that had become a habit with me. He looked at me strangely and said, "Nice girls don't talk like that." He never asked me out again. His rebuke jolted my conscience and from then on I cut that type of thing out of my conversation.

Happily enough, there are still men about who consider women special and treat them that way. They don't hide behind the old man's tale that "Women ain't ladies no more, so I ain't bein' no gennulman." I suspect any man who feels that way was never a gentleman in the first place.

Being a real man will have a tremendous effect on your children, too. God help us if all our children see in us is a lust-laden, weak generation that is so desperate for acceptance it has to smoke, drink, commit adultery and curse in order to gain it. Then what was once a bid for acceptance eventually becomes a motivation for living. The kids are sickened by it, and turned off, even though they follow right along in the "venerated" footsteps.

RIGHTS REGGIE has a schedule in his mind. He feels he has a right to sex with his wife four times a week and if he doesn't get it, he is furious. It's no wonder his wife is developing headaches, backaches, frequent bouts of fever and anything else she can think of to avoid her "duty."

A counselor tells of one poor fellow who came into his office distraught because he wasn't getting what he felt was his due. The conversation went something like this:

"Do you know how many times a week the average American couple has sex?" (His voice was rising.) The counselor didn't know. He had only scanned the official report that had been making news. The fellow leaned over the desk, his face red, his fist clenched as it came down on the ink blotter. "Two and seven-tenths times, that's what!" he gritted out, "and I'm only getting it two and two-tenths times." The poor misguided soul committed suicide some time later, unable to adjust to his wife or life.

When your mental processes begin to tell you that you have to guard against being cheated out of your "rights" you've lost a good portion of the battle. Now is the time to use that extraordinary male computer of a brain to program your reactions differently.

Doris's marriage to Bill is as fresh and exciting as it was when they were married. Even more so. It's as if the honeymoon has never stopped. Wise husband that he is, he never INSISTS that they make love because as he says, "If my wife is anxious to have me make love to her, I will enjoy it more because she's enjoying it. Her response will be passionate, not just submissive. I want an exciting woman and she is. So we never count the times. Sometimes it is two or three times a week. Sometimes it is two or three times a month. Whichever, it is always a thrill. We've never let it become cheapened by routine."

You may respond, "If I were to let it go like that, my wife wouldn't ever let me near her." If you've read these first five chapters carefully and are working on the suggestions there, and if you read the following chapter with an open mind and put it to use, that won't be the case at all—in time. Instead, you will have a willing bed partner and your enjoyment will be increased a hundredfold.

One more word about Bill and Doris. When it is not possible for them to come together for a lengthy period of time, Bill continues his romancing of her. He never withholds his wooing. If he were to turn it on or turn it off according to when he wants sex, she would turn off and not respond.

Opposite to Bill is Jerry. He likes to have sex every morning, every noon and every night. The young wife said, "I don't really mind that as long as he doesn't expect me to have a climax every time." What she really is saying is, "I'll put up with it, but I can't respond or enjoy it." Foolish, foolish young man. He's like a spoiled child who must have candy every day, and he will cry and pout if he doesn't get it. The time will come when that young wife will find excuses. She'll either develop psychosomatic illnesses to escape this eager one who refuses to romance her and uphold her as an individual, or they'll get a divorce. They were already seeking counseling, and the trouble was just beginning.

> *BORING BRAD* never uses his imagination and his wife is too shy to do so. Lovemaking is done in the same place, at the same time, on the same days every week.

Such a routine can kill romance and thus love. Keep in mind that if you ate hamburgers every day, year in and year out, you would get sick of hamburgers. A young love that lasts for 50 years needs variety. Creative lovemaking may seem shocking to you and your wife at first, especially if both of you haven't been freely enjoying each other, but *after* your wife begins to adore you because of all the new things you are going to try with her, you can get on with some imaginative times together. For instance, if your business allows, get away for lunch and come home (make a romantic date with her the day before), planning time enough to eat leisurely and to make love leisurely. If you can't arrange it during the week, make arrangements for the children to visit someone occasionally on Saturday for a few hours and have your special time then. Although bed is a nice place to be, it isn't the only place. Consider enjoying each other in front of a crackling fire, with romantic records playing, or charm her in the living room where you've placed the rosebuds you brought her. Once your wife becomes responsive, she'll have a few suggestions of her own. One obstetrician's advice to women patients is never to make love at night when they are weary. He does not say it to the older women for he has found them so set in their ways, so critical and "shocked" at anything different that they do not respond to any suggestions. These women need to be educated and made to feel young, beautiful and adventurous again by their husbands.

> NO-EXCUSE CHARLIE is a man who will have his playtime regardless! He has a wife who is ill quite often, but that makes no difference to Charlie. That's just her tough luck. Nobody is going to stop him. Charlie is the kind who will have his sex even if his wife has a fever. He is totally inconsiderate and hasn't an ounce of compassion in him that's noticeable. But watch what happens if Charlie ever gets sick. He's irritable, he's demanding, and expects to be waited on hand and foot.

This world is full of sickness and many wives are suffering legitimately from one illness or another. A man married to such a woman needs a lot of self-control, and he can have it if he wants to be truly considerate and not make her life more miserable by insisting she perform when she isn't capable.

In Sickness or in Health

One of the biggest complaints of wives is that they are tired. If you hear your wife complaining about being tired for any length of time, and especially as soon as she gets up in the morning, don't pass it off with a shrug and a "not that routine again" look. It may be the signal that could save her life or keep her from a fatal disease later on, if you pay attention to it. I went through this syndrome for several years and, although it didn't affect my physical relationship with my husband, it wasn't easy to be as tired when I got up as when I went to bed. When a few other symptoms developed, I went in for a complete physical. The doctor pronounced me perfectly healthy, saying I was just chronically exhausted. I was to get more rest. More rest seemed an impossibility and deep inside I felt sure his diagnosis was not complete. Some time later, I went to another doctor who is noted for his more extensive and thorough physical examinations. When I was finished there, I knew what every organ in my body was doing and why. One of the main problems was a poisoned liver and hypoglycemia (low blood sugar) which, surprisingly, is brought on by stress.[3]

Stress is present in all lives and can be generally placed in four categories:

> nutritional
> emotional
> physical
> chemical

Some bodies can handle more stress than others, but if anyone has too much stress to deal with, he begins to lose the battle for good health.

Nutritional stress is brought about by a wrong diet punctuated with a heavy intake of carbohydrates (sugar and foods that turn to sugar) and stimulants, as well as the eating of refined foods.

Emotional stress comes from such sources as quarreling, worry, anger, fear, sorrow, excitement, etc.

[3]All medical information in this chapter was derived from Alan H. Nittler, M.D., author of *A New Breed of Doctor* (see Bibliography).

Physical stress comes into being through overexertion and inadequate rest.

Among *chemicals* the body has to fight are preservatives, impurities in the air and additives to our food and water.

One doctor estimates that 80% of the people walking on the street have hypoglycemia (men and women). It was causing my exhaustion. Hypoglycemia can contribute to the cause of practically any undesirable condition, including serious diseases. So the answer was to begin the process of cutting down on the various stresses. What resulted in me, over years of abuse, may be the basic root of your wife's problems.

One friend, wife of a radio station manager, had suicidal tendencies and great periods of depression, suffering with it for some twelve years before an observant physician insisted she have a Five-Hour Glucose Tolerance Test and discovered that indeed she had hypoglycemia. Setting forth a periodic cleansing program for her body, putting her on a no-stimulant, low-carbohydrate diet, urging her to eat foods as close to the "natural" state as possible, plus more rest made a new woman out of her.

Among my acquaintances alone, I know of numerous women and men who have low blood sugar. It is a serious condition, fairly easy to detect with the proper test and not difficult to control.

A Time For Tenderness

Another major setback to happy physical union is premenstrual troubles. Most women have up to a week of tension, backaches, and depression before their menstrual period begins. If they have an illness, like hypoglycemia, it will be even worse unless their health is built up. One survey reported that of all the women incarcerated in prisons, most of the crimes they committed were done during that week. Your wife needs you to be tender during that time and very tolerant when she is unreasonable or "impossible." Instead of looking at her as though she escaped from somewhere and saying, "What's the matter with you?" a wise husband checks the calendar he keeps on which he marks the expected dates of her period, perhaps putting large X's on each day for a week preceding it. He will encourage his wife to be extra patient and sweet during this time while he is being the same with her. He will sympathize with her if she is tired or suffering cramps. He and she will stand in awe of this normal, natural and wonderful process of eliminating from her system the preparation her body has made for having a baby which she is not having. This wise husband will not expect his wife to indulge in sexual intercourse during the time of her period unless she requests it, for her body is very weak and tender inside. If you are providing enough romance in your wife's life in the other areas mentioned thus far, she will not play on your emotions and overdo her "discomforts" during this time.

If you have a teen-age daughter, you have double duty to perform. She's going to need special patience from you at this time too, and also a respect for her privacy and modesty.

You may have a real challenge if your wife is going through the menopause. Some women have a very difficult time, although one doctor told me that a perfectly healthy woman should have no trouble at all. The problem is, there are very few perfectly healthy women. By the time they reach that stage in their lives, their eating and working habits will have weakened their resistance considerably. This will be a real test of your love. Some men walk out on their wives at this stage, when they need them the most. It's almost more than a woman can bear, and I have seen some turn into hags when the horrible burden of losing their husbands is placed upon them.

HURRYING HARRY will never be a good lover. He doesn't know the first thing about his wife's needs nor does he care. He hasn't enough self-control to think beyond his own wants.

And this brings us to the nitty-gritty of lovemaking, which every man thinks he knows everything about. But our survey pointed out emphatically that the wives didn't agree with their husbands on this point at all. The husbands considered themselves good lovers, generally. The majority of the women felt their husbands were "in need of instruction" or were "clumsy." Evidently these women, judging by the husband's answers, were keeping the truth from their men to keep peace in the family. In fact, the men reported that their wives were experiencing an orgasm to a much greater extent than the women reported. So swallow your pride and forget your male ego for a little bit. Let's see if we can't light some fires that have been out for some time.

*

.P.S. Wife, your husband may not even see himself in his proper role here. No need to ire him by giving him a label like Critical Curtis. It's just as easy to say softly, "Sweetheart, it upsets me when you do that. Please don't." And when he begins to make some changes, be liberal with the appreciation, all right?

6

Sex—Wow or Drag?

Most men would like to satisfy their wives but they are stymied as to how to do it. Many women accept their role as a passive partner, taking pleasure only in the fact that their husbands are enjoying it. Perhaps that has been your case, but I hope from this day forward neither you nor your wife will ever be satisfied with that again. For not only is she being cheated out of something thrilling, but your enjoyment is lessened considerably because it is one-sided.

Who has ever watched a glorious sunset or a deer suddenly dart out of the bushes in the forest, or felt the tug of a heavy trout on a line that he hasn't wanted to turn and share it with someone? All things are enjoyed more if they are shared. Man was meant to share. He is not generally a loner. God made man to want and need other human beings. After Admiral Byrd spent those days alone in the Antarctic, he stated that the worst thing he had to endure was the loneliness of being away from other human beings. Even more than other human beings, God created most men to need a female as a partner. He intended her to round him out, and to make him complete. It was not good that man should be alone. He was to share with her all his life.

And since God very ingeniously invented sex, not only as a means of propogating the race, but as a delightful experience, it was in His plan for the woman to get as much out of it as the man. If this were not so, He would never have given her the organs which give her pleasurable sensations and bring her to the ecstasy of the orgasm. The Victorian idea is not around much anymore, but it is surprising how many people still feel that sex must be naughty, that enjoying the nakedness of your mate is outrageously sinful and that women should lie still as logs while their husbands attempt a relationship. The mother of a dear ninety-year-old friend of mine once said proudly to her, "Your father has never seen above my elbows." No bare skin revealed there! And they had four children! Don't point at the church. All these people are not in the church.

Just as unbelievable to the opposite extreme are those who are so desperately afraid they'll miss out on something that they resort to lewdness, feed their minds on pornographic material and attempt to bring into their marriage relationships the abominable practices of the masters of pornography whose ideas are spawned in hell itself. As we saw when we observed Crude Corey, this type of approach is deadly to the emotions and sensivitity of the female makeup. Women who participate in these types of practices confess they experience little or no pleasure from them.

Nor does promiscuity increase one's *knowledge* of

sexual enjoyment. One young woman was in tears as she sat before the counselor. She had indulged in sexual experiences with many young men, seeking satisfaction, but finding none. She had never had an orgasm. None of these young men, in their selfish desire to satisfy only themselves on a quick and temporary basis, had the slightest interest in whether she enjoyed it or not.

Some women feel compelled to secretly masturbate to obtain relief because their husbands are not willing to take the necessary steps to bring them satisfaction. It is sad that anyone feels compelled to resort to this practice. It shows once again a society woefully lacking in proper human relationships.

Valentino or Gable?

The great lovers of history need have nothing on you. At this you may laugh long and loud and say, "If she thinks I'm going to try to become a great lover at this stage of the game. . . ." May I ask why not? If not a great lover, at least you can be a better one than you have been in the past. And of course, if you have had problems in this area, it behooves you all the more to take the bull by the horns and wrestle this problem down until it is underfoot.

Your chest may have slipped and your hair may have flown with the wind, but inside that flesh which has changed through the years is still YOU—masculine, handsome, dashing, strong, appealing YOU! The reason your wife doesn't recognize the fact is that you have been keeping it hidden behind an unexciting, boring personality, at least toward her. Of course, you will be that much ahead if you do something about that slipped chest. On a cruise my husband and I enjoyed, we were amused and amazed to see hundreds of vacationing men and women with bulging bellies. What a picture the American traveler presents in the ports of other countries!

It's Not That Difficult

One of the first things you should do, if you and your wife communicate well, is to choose an evening when she is relaxed and happy, especially now that she is beginning to see you are trying to supply the romance and kindness in her life that she craves. Sit down with her and explain that you are going to attempt to be a better lover, too. Ask her to please be patient with you as you will no doubt bumble and make mistakes, but you want her to enjoy your love life together as much as you do and you are going to work toward that goal no matter how long it takes. She may not react with enthusiasm at all, for she may have given up and become discouraged herself, or she may be so hardened and bitter that she won't readily accept trying all over again. Her shattered dreams won't easily repair themselves.

But don't *you* be easily discouraged. One pastor told me that for 17 years his wife had never experienced an orgasm. Since he loved her dearly and wanted her to enjoy the relationship as much as himself, he went to doctors and other professional men, seeking an answer. Alas, they were as ignorant on the matter as he was, which is proving a lot about what we are saying, is it not? Then one day he discovered what was causing the problem. It was a very simple thing really and the result is she has been enjoying her sexual experiences for 25 years. We'll discuss what he discovered very shortly in this chapter. I trust it won't take you 17 years to find out what is causing your problem.

Secondly, you and your wife should read a good book on the physical relationship of marriage, out loud, together. Your local librarian can recommend some. George and I read two before our wedding day and they helped us both get off to a good start. We spent several evenings together, reading and discussing the material. George, as well as I, learned a great deal neither of us knew before. It served another purpose as well. The actual wedding night was met without embarrassment or trauma, for we both understood what we expected of each other. Two excellent volumes recommended by counselors and psychologists are: *Sex Without Fear* by S. A. Lewin, M.D., and John Gilmore, Ph.D., and *Sexual Happiness in Marriage* by Herbert J. Miles, Ph.D. These books tell in detail what I can only touch on in this chapter. But perhaps I might pass on a few basic pointers that most men should know and practice but don't.

Prepare! Prepare! Prepare!

The majority of women I've talked with and who answered our survey questionnaire felt their husbands did not prepare them enough and some stated flatly that they aren't prepared at all. This preparation, which is essential if your wife is going to enjoy your union to the fullest, should be a continuing thing, never ending, whether you are anticipating sexual intercourse or not. But it can be concentrated somewhat when you are looking forward to intimate relations with your wife. As a sensitive creature she must never be made to feel that you are using her only for your own physical satisfaction. Women resent this. One woman said, "I do refuse him sometimes because I feel he is just using me. He never prepares me, or cares about me. He just wants relief and I resent that." She needs to feel, above all, that you care about her welfare and enjoyment, even above your own.

If Wednesday night is what you have in mind, you might hold her tenderly on Tuesday night and say, "How about a date tomorrow?" If she says no, try another night as soon as the reason she is giving is gone. Or you might put it like this, "I'd like to make love to you tomorrow night, honey." If your communication has been sorry in the past or even if it hasn't, you might begin with, "Sweetheart, I want a date with you Saturday night. Dinner at Petro's. Just the two of us. And I'd love to have you wear that long blue dress."

As Wednesday or Saturday approaches, do thoughtful things for her: help her with the dinner; kiss her tenderly, sometimes briefly, longer if she responds. Admire her out loud. Of course, you don't want to overdo. One man in his 60s who had lived with a turned-off wife for many years, finally got the counsel he needed and decided to go about the business of turning her on. I was visiting in their home overnight and was amused at his loud attempts to change things. "That's my sweetheart, there," he boomed to us all. "She's a real hot number, she is," and similar phrases that would have been better for her ears alone. Being introverted and shy, you could almost see her wilt. Don't be phony. Be sincere.

In the mornings before you leave, hold her and kiss her a few times. If she's still in curlers and a sloppy bathrobe, you may have to steel yourself a bit until you've conquered that part of her. She will start trying to improve that if you follow the right strategy. If possible, on Wednesday call her just to tell her you love her and to wish her a nice day. You might drop a hint that you'd like to see her wearing that little yellow dress you like so much when you get home.

When you enter the door with a smile on your face, even if the roast is burning and she didn't bother with the yellow dress, greet her with a whirl around the room or a hug and kiss, telling her you love her, or saying, "I'm glad to be home with you, Sweetheart." Or in light of the burned roast, "Don't worry about it, honey. Let's go out to dinner."

Even as the children clamor for your attention, you can look at her and wink, or reach out and touch her hand. You can say, "Look, children, don't you have a pretty mama?" Since my husband has made a practice of treating me ideally through the years, my teen-age son has picked it up. It isn't unusual for him to greet me with, "Hello, my beautiful Mom," or say,

"Mom, I just love you so much," and like phrases. And he often jumps to help me.

No Room For Resentment

After dinner help her get the kids to bed and the dishes done. No wife is going to be a willing bed partner if she is worn out or if you sit down in front of the TV and your paper while she labors on through the evening after a long day.

Patty married young and eagerly. Her three small children are very lively. She's married to a fellow who invariably enters the door complaining about someone or something. He eats dinner with very little comment about its excellence. Then it's TV and the paper while she cleans up the dinner mess. Occasionally he yells at her to come get one of the kids who is bothering him. By the time she has the three children bathed and in bed, she is exhausted and wants a little time to herself. She plans a relaxing bath and hopes to read a little in the book she's been saving. At that point, he either gets angry or pouts, for he is ready for bed and he always expects playtime when he goes night-night. So she gives in to prevent trouble. But he's the only one who considers it play. He never bothers to prepare her at all, and five or ten minutes later he is satisfied, and she's disgusted. Their marriage is becoming full of friction and they bicker a great deal. He chafes that she argues with him and doesn't submit to his authority as head of the house. She isn't as pretty as she used to be, and the bounce has gone out of her step. She is also developing numerous physical ailments and sicknesses.

But you, the one who will win your wife as the knight wins a princess, won't be such a clod. You've already helped her with the dishes and anything else that needs doing. The children are tucked into bed, kissed and prayed with.

Now is where your genius can start operating.

Try It; You'll Like It

There are many things you can do to put your wife in the right frame of mind, and what you decide on for Wednesday night, you may exchange for something else on Saturday night.

You must keep in mind once again that woman is not as physical in her approach as man is. You get turned on by the sight of physically attractive women, or a pair of legs. You are ready for sex if your wife kisses you passionately. You feel excitement at just the thought of a naked body inside a filmy nightgown. But she reacts very differently. She may admire your body, but a man's torso does not generally affect a woman by arousing her sexually. She loves to see you in good looking clothes, but just looking at you will not get her excited. A passionate kiss from you probably won't either, especially if it is ill-timed. Her desires will be aroused by the little romantic things you are going to put into practice right away. She may instigate the lovemaking once in awhile, which is right and good, but you were created the pursuer, she the pursued, and basically that responsibility will be yours.

Here are ideas which you may use. Try some on Wednesday; others on Saturday. Make up a few of your own for the following Tuesday.

1. Draw her bath if she hasn't had one yet. Put bubbles in it. Maybe she would like to have you wash her back.
2. Always (regardless of the day) bathe yourself. Put on cologne, brush your teeth (yes, again), comb your hair, shave, unless you wear a beard (you never wore stubble in your dating days). Get an attractive wrap-around garment to wear instead of the same old white shorts she's been seeing for years.
3. Don't come at her naked and passionate. This is okay at rare moments, but you are likely to be

the one who will feel passion rise because of it, not she.

4. If you have brought her a bouquet of flowers from the supermarket or the garden, bring them into the room, and light a candle next to them.
5. Have soft music playing—the kind she likes.
6. Pick a flower and put it in her hair.
7. Massage her feet (no tickling please) or kiss them.
8. Massage her back, brushing her neck and back with your lips.
9. Brush her hair (unless she has a set hairdo).
10. Bring her a special fruit drink or hot drink depending on weather. Remember, alcohol can defeat your purpose altogether. The sugar in it can have the same effect as coffee—it gives a lift and then later, a sudden drop. She may become so relaxed with this depressant that it will be difficult to arouse her.
11. Let her talk over her troubles; sympathize but don't argue. If she gets started on a wrong subject, kiss it away and suggest you discuss it tomorrow.
12. Share some things with her—not controversial or anything to arouse her jealousy.
13. Undress her slowly before she takes her bath, complimenting her on how beautiful her body is to you. Allow her to keep some covering if it makes her feel better.
14. If she wishes, let her undress you.
15. Sing a love song to her.
16. Say lots of sweet things.

Whatever you do, don't rush her. A man who thinks five minutes is enough preparation is kidding himself. That length of time is welcome only to the woman who isn't enjoying her experience anyway and wants to get it over with. Be prepared to take *whatever time* is necessary. Let her decide and you react accordingly.

Generally, 20 minutes to a half hour is realistic,

if she is in the habit of reaching a climax, but 45 minutes to an hour may be necessary as you start to discover each other all over again.

Sometimes women like to be handled passionately, and sometimes gently. You'll have to heed your understanding and her response concerning that. But usually a good rule is to keep your caresses gentle until her passions begin to rise. Her intimate parts shouldn't be approached right away either. The body is a beautiful thing to behold and to caress. If your wife has a block about you touching any part of her body or about her touching any part of your body, she needs to be released from her unnatural fears, for her reluctance is no virtue. Indeed, certain parts of her body have to be caressed at length, with her willing participation, if she is ever to enjoy sexual arousement and the final delight of the orgasm.

The Secret.

So we come to the secret discovered by the pastor whose wife did not experience a climax in their first 17 years of marriage. This man of God now provides all his counselees with a diagram of the male and female bodies and points out the different parts and their functions. He is constantly amazed at how ignorant grown people are in this time when sex education is so prevalent. As he shows his diagram, he points to the clitoris in the woman's body, a small organ just above the urethra near the entrance to the vagina. It corresponds to the man's penis somewhat. He points out that it is not as easily stimulated as its male counterpart, but it is essential that you become adept at manipulating, gently massaging it, patiently and at length, before actual intercourse. Although some women receive adequate massaging of the clitoris during intercourse, many do not for the size of this organ varies in women. In some, it is very small.

In others, it might be as large as one-half inch in length. A woman's breasts are also a point of contact for sexual arousement, especially the nipples. They should not be handled roughly, unless she indicates to you that this is what she desires. A combination of massaging the clitoris and the nipples coupled with much kissing and continued caressing of the entire body, will bring her to the point of signaling when she is ready for the penetration of the penis. Although her glands will have bathed the vagina in a mucous to provide for the entrance of the penis, it is still wise to enter slowly and carefully unless she suggests otherwise, for sometimes discomfort is felt.

During intercourse, it is very important that you not ejaculate before your wife experiences her orgasm. She needs your passion in order to continue hers as well as the firmness of the penis. If you cannot control your responses once the act has begun, it might be better for you to bring her to an orgasm through manual manipulation as mentioned before, until you can learn to regulate yourself.

When the pastor, formerly mentioned, realized what he needed to do, it wasn't long until his wife experienced that "moment of ecstacy," as he calls it. He realizes that people who are afraid or shocked to discuss these matters for any reason are liable to be headed for marital disaster in this age when divorce papers flow free and easy.

One of man's fears is that his sexual organs might be too small. Somehow, the size of the male organs is equated with masculinity in some men's minds. That should not be. However, if this is the case, admit it, but realize also that your wife's vagina may be too large. Once again the solution might be to bring her to her climax before the actual act, or at least to the very brink. Or, if you are very adept, you may be able to manipulate the clitoris during the act of intercourse, not ejaculating until you are sure she has reached her orgasm. It is not essential, in any case, for both of you to reach a climax at the same time. The idea is nice, but it doesn't seem to heighten the enjoyment on either side.

Practice Control

Remember, just as being able to control your temper is a mark of maturity, so is being able to control your sexual responses. To do so, you must truly desire to put your wife's needs before your own. As you sincerely try, time and time again, for as long as it takes to gain your control and bring about the desired response in your wife, she will soon be doing all she can to help you, and will appreciate your sacrifice more than you will ever know.

If your wife rejects your attempts to make love, you must not feel it is a rejection of *you* or your *manliness.* If you have followed the suggestions mentioned in this book and the suggestions yet to come (looking at it from her viewpoint), and she still rejects you, look upon it as *her* problem—a problem that you are going to help her solve because you love her and are concerned that she is being limited in her pleasure.

If your wife thinks she and you are "too old" for "that sort of thing," she's not being honest or is ignorant. The pastor we have continued to talk about is now in his 70s, as is his wife, and they are getting as much out of their sex life as ever. Women who have the mistaken idea that sexual intercourse is only for the childbearing age and then it must stop, are women who have never really liked it, I suspect, or have a distorted sense of what the Bible teaches on the subject. Proverbs 5:19 says, "Let her (thy wife) be as the loving hind and pleasant roe; let her breasts satisfy thee at all times and be thou ravished always with her love."

If God had intended sexual pleasure to stop with the beginning or cessation of the menopause, He would have caused the organs that supply pleasure to discontinue their function as well.

A good Scripture for these same people might be the one which says, "Marriage is honorable in all, and the bed undefiled. . . ." Hebrews 13:4. Most Christian authorities in the field of marriage relations agree that this indicates that there is no technique or position or practice that is wrong for those who are married and making love in harmony. Lawrence J. Crabb, Jr. Ph.D., states: "The Bible nowhere specifies that husband and wife may not engage in any particular sex practice."[4] May I caution you, however, that abnormal behavior, such as cruelty, or many of those suggested by the pornographers, will be repugnant to anyone with a conscience of decency and shouldn't be forced on one partner by another.

A Very Wise Man

Song of Solomon, found in the Old Testament, and written by a man noted for the extraordinary wisdom given him by God, is a beautiful spiritual gem as it describes Christ's relationship to the church. The analogy is explained by a bride-bridegroom relationship and has some excellent hints for lovers who would be successful. It points out vividly how a woman will respond, given the proper treatment.

The bridegroom in this account has his lady's number. He knows how to make her happy. He uses lots of words and whispers many sweet nothings. He compares her with a beautiful garden where he can enjoy the loveliest of flowers and fragrances. His garden is full of beautiful refreshments. He also compares her, in his marvelous masculine way, with various animals which he admires greatly—magnificent horses, beautiful goats and charming doves. Had he said she reminded him of the old cow down in the "South Forty," I don't believe she would have responded enthusiastically. No, he makes his comparisons carefully.

He speaks as lovingly of her navel and her thighs as

he does her neck, her lips and her hair. He is delighted with her.

She has a few things to say about him, as well. She speaks of his entire body as glorious to her. Their lovemaking is in full appreciation of each other's charms, for the bridegroom says, "How fair and how pleasant art thou, O love, for delights! This thy stature is like a palm tree, and thy breasts, to clusters of grapes. I will go up to the palm tree, I will take hold of its boughs; now also thy breasts shall be like clusters of the vine; and the fragrance of thy breath like apples, and the roof of thy mouth, like the best wine."

The bride answers proudly, "I am my beloved's and his desire is toward me. Come, my beloved, let us go forth into the field; let us lodge in the villages; let us get up early in the vineyards . . . There will I give thee my love. His mouth is most sweet, yea, he is altogether lovely."

She finds him so impelling and delightful that she hates to be separated from him, even for the day! She looks her loveliest for him, putting on her best perfumes and garments. He takes her places, including banquets, all the time filling her ears and heart with the things she wants to hear. Her whole life is given over to him, because she adores him. She is emotionally bolstered by her husband, so she comes across to others as a strong woman, commanding respect. She is admired by all. She becomes homesick, so the bridegroom takes her home to visit her relatives. Then he declares with great solemnity the strength of love.

It is tragic that Solomon departed from this wisdom, acquiring hundreds of wives and concubines. This led to his downfall and severe punishment. But you need not fall into the same trap. Your little woman can become ravishingly beautiful in your estimation of her if you apply the earlier wisdom of Solomon to your relationship.

*

P.S. Madame, no man can become a fantastic lover without a responsive woman. If you only realized how many women are out there just dying to get their hands on your husband! So

1) Set your mind right. Be determined to enjoy your sexual times with your man.
2) Help him. Let him know what he's doing right and very gently what he's doing wrong. Start to live!

7

Help!

"This house is a mess!" There! You've said it. The house usually looks like a disaster area and you have done one of two things about it: not said anything at all or complained with no noticeable results. Both approaches are wrong.

Mike was a "nice guy" sort of husband. His wife was the creative sort, strong in personality and fun to be with. When she cried, she howled. When she laughed, she roared. When she cleaned, she slaved. When she played she really played. Whatever she did, it was to an extreme. The difficulty was that she didn't keep a happy balance between her extremes. As a consequence, some weeks she played while the house went to pot. Other weeks she cleaned up a storm. The problem was, she played more than she

cleaned and the house showed it. Actually it was the
mess that was tough to take. Her unfinished ceramics
dominated the family room. Her sewing never was
put away in the den, her art filled the garage, and
she never seemed to get her clothes hung up.

Be Honest

Mike, quiet and not willing to disturb the waters,
adjusted to his wife as best as he could. He learned to
shove the pans aside when he made himself a sand-
wich. He rationalized that a messy house need not
mean a dirty one, and besides, didn't he have a happy
wife? No, really he didn't. Not totally. All of us need
discipline. Even the things his wife liked to do were
frustrating to her, because she had never learned
to be organized in her approach to her work. She was
forever looking for her glue, or her pins or her best
slip. So it was, 18 years later, that his wife was thun-
derstruck when Mike walked out on her. Counseling
revealed that she had no idea he was fed up with
the mess. He had never told her, which he admitted.
He wasn't honest with his wife.

The particular counselor involved in this case told
me that she felt lack of honesty was the biggest
problem in marriages that aren't making it. Being able
to talk to your mate about the things that bother
you is vitally important. But hold on there, you manly
type who usually "tells it like it is." There is a way!
There is a way to be honest without hurting either
your mate or yourself. A woman that is pounced on
about her faults is not going to like it, no matter how
you spell t-r-u-t-h. Only a few can take it, and usually
they do because they're afraid of their husbands. That
approach should be relegated to the Dark Ages where
it belongs.

Our survey revealed that almost without exception,
the husbands felt they took criticism from their wives
in a mature manner. Conversely, the wives felt the

same about themselves. But the husbands generally felt that the wives could *not* take criticism well, and the wives said the same thing about their husbands. To quote Robert Burns:

> "Oh wad some power the giftie gie us
> To see oursels as others see us! . . ."
>
> From *Familiar Quotations*

Be Mature

When I was first married, I was not a good housekeeper. I kept things clean, but I never could keep the house neat. My background and temperament, although no excuse, both had something to do with it. My high school and college years were spent getting an education, pursuing my music and dramatic career and rushing off to this place or that. My folks didn't insist on my keeping things in order.

Since opposites attract, so the man I married happened to be very neat, concise and organized as many men are. Now he had a problem. Not only was I a poor housekeeper, but I was easily upset when criticized. That's an incendiary situation! But I was about to learn my first lesson in just how mature and masculine men can be! George didn't yell at me. He didn't harp and berate. Nor did he complain to others about it. Instead, each evening when he came home, he would quietly clean everything. Nor did he give me dirty looks or act like he held it against me. He was sweet and loving. He showed me through his actions that he did not like the way I was keeping house, but there was no way I could get on the defensive about it. The Bible says, "A soft answer turneth away wrath, but grievous words stir up anger."

It took about six months. I was beginning to feel thoroughly ashamed of myself. The realization that I had a responsibility began to work itself into my thinking. I began to learn to keep house. It was not an easy process. Some people have a natural bent toward neatness. My natural bents were toward drama, music and writing—not organizing housework. Now, I love my house neat and clean at all times, if possible, and it is my husband who insists I quit and get on with my creative endeavors!

Few men would consider that sort of approach. They would rather battle it out, day after day, year after year, butting their heads against a stone wall then use the wits and will to win.

How often I've seen young husbands prefer to sit down in a messy house than get in and help their wives clean.

Taking care of a home, children and husband is not an easy task. A husband walks into the house and says to his wife, "I don't understand why you can't get this done. All you have to do all day is the house." Visions of the thousand interruptions she suffered will dance through her head, and not like sugarplums, either. Accidents and emergencies will loom to the front as she thinks back over the day, the events being too numerous to recall. The overwhelming job she has will suddenly become totally impossible in her thinking because you, the man she wants approval from the most, did not understand. Truthfully speaking, I have to agree that most men don't realize what a tremendously big job a woman faces, especially if she has children living at home. And doubly so if the children are of preschool age. Let me run through a very possible day in the life of a young mother with children, ages one and three.

6:00 A.M. Baby awakens earlier than usual. Wife changes her, gives her toys and bottle. Runs to get three-year-old balancing precariously on kitchen counter, getting cereal. Waters him, gives him book and cracker. Tucks him back into bed.

6:45 Wife climbs wearily back into bed.

7:00 Alarm rings. Husband and wife jump up. Husband begins grooming for day. Wife races off in curlers and robe. Three-year-old is screaming—fallen out of crib. Baby sets up howl (she's hungry).

7:30 Husband rushes into kitchen. Wife stirring scrambled eggs with baby under arm, three-year-old tugging at robe. Husband gasps, "Where's the coffee?" Forgot to put it on. He is not happy. Wife makes quick cup of instant, scalds her hand, plops baby in high chair.

Baby throws cereal on floor. Three-year-old spills milk.

7:38 Wife cleans mess. Husband yells at three-year-old, baby and wife.

7:50 Breakfast done, husband finds wife under curlers, pecks her, races out door. She chokes down breakfast. Fixes hand.

8:30 Kids are mopped up. Baby in playpen. Three-year-old banging pans. Wife tackles dishes.

The next two hours are a blur of happenings: changing diapers; taking three-year-old to potty; putting three-year-old outside, all bundled up; bringing three-year-old inside, unbundling him; letting dog out; letting dog in; answering telephone; answering door; getting bean out of baby's nose; kissing a hurt; repairing a toy; forgetting the dirty clothes and on and on and on.

10:30 Back at the dishes. Three-year-old wants cookie. Baby throws up on floor. Next two hours another blur of happenings.

12:45 Dishes finally done. Children yelling for lunch. Curlers falling out. Bathrobe dirtier.

The afternoon is a repeat performance with slight changes. An hour before husband gets home, everything breaks loose and the time she had hoped to spend in the tub and fixing herself up is spent repairing a skinned nose, helping a neighbor find her lost little girl and trying to figure out something for dinner. She manages to get out of her bathrobe but three-year-old wipes jelly on her clean dress.

Homecoming

He walks in! He looks around. What a mess! What's the matter with her? What a lousy housekeeper. His mother was never like this. The meal is something less than what he desires, which he comments about, and after dinner when he is trying to concentrate on his newspaper, there she is rattling dishes and yelling at the children.

Even worse, when he is ready for bed and wants a little of what he deserves, he gets it. She complains of a headache. She is tired. She doesn't want to, not tonight. He is disgusted.

Happily, not all days are like that, but it doesn't take very many of them to convince a woman that all days *are* like that. When the children start to school, she will be able to manage a little better. But there still will be THOSE days, and some women will never improve much without help . . . from you . . . strong, practical, mind-over-matter YOU.

Give Her a Day Off

Before you can start reforming her, you have got to convince her that you are interested in her welfare above all. She has got to feel that you understand. She should have at least one day a week all to herself to do what she wants. "A day off!" screams the husband. "She can't do the job working all seven! I should give her a day off?" Tell me honestly. How would you like to work at your job seven days a week without a day off? Hmmm? And how about the hours? Hers may start at 6:00 A.M. and not end until 11:00 P.M. Is that the kind of hours you would like to work at the same job? Of course not. Just for the sake of her sanity, if nothing else, she needs to get away from it all.

Her day can be on Saturday while you stay with the children, if you are short on money. Or even better, a day during the week. Hire a capable woman to come in to watch the children or to be there when they get home from school. This will be Mama's day off and it will hold a special magic even for the kids if the attitude is right about it.

My day off was Saturday, because that was the only day I could have a studio for recording my daily radio program.[5] I did five or six programs a week. George stayed at home with the children. He has, time without number, expressed his gratitude for those years. Not only did it give me a break from the children and the house, but it gave him a wonderful opportunity to become a real father. He usually spent the day working outside, with the children beside him. In our home movies, one picture is so precious to me. It shows our two-year-old son lifting a full-size saw and trying to cut wood with it. The baby would be in a box in the wheelbarrow with rocks that she could take out and throw, "helping Daddy." Our children learned to work at a very early age, you might say. Oh, sometimes they went with wet pants too long, or didn't get their food and naps on time, but the lessons they learned on Saturdays were far more important. Today, my teen-age son works like a full-grown man and puts out a long, hard day's labor every Saturday. He and his Dad still look forward to the excitement of that day together. It meant that George couldn't get nearly as much done on those days when they were little, but he never lost his patience in showing them how to do things and keeping them constantly busy and happy "working." Another benefit was that it made him sympathetic toward my difficulties in getting things accomplished.

A neighbor said to me once, "My husband can hardly wait until our son gets to be Vance's age, so he can work with him like George does with your boy." Vance was seven years old at that time. What our neighbor failed to realize is, if you wait until they are the "right" age the years will be gone and you still won't have spent time with them doing the things you should, teaching the things they ought to be learning. You need to start when they are tiny. If you make it a fun thing, they will never dislike work and when they are older they will be of real help to you. George was able to enjoy seeing firsthand all the delightful, precious things that little children do and say that most fathers only get secondhand.

Me? Help?

Our survey shows that most men are willing to do dishes some of the time and certain other small household chores once in awhile to help their wives. But most draw the line if it gets into any major hunk of time. George never has left me to do the work alone after dinner. I've never asked him to help me with any part of the housework. I never have to. He always cheerfully helps me, realizing that my strength is gone at the end of the day. In fact, the whole family works together on most nights and has the kitchen clean in ten minutes. George makes a game or contest of it. He lends his strength to me because he loves me. I will try never to take advantage of that, because I love him. I will attempt to keep his house clean and neat, the way he likes it.

Figure It Out

Generally, a woman will listen to suggestions for more efficient housekeeping from her husband IF the husband is not criticizing her, and IF she feels he understands her situation. One sure way to have a very resentful wife after awhile is to sit and relax in the evenings while she has to work on and on. But there are timesaving hints that everyone can learn. My husband taught me several and I have picked up a few myself:

Everyone: never leave a room without taking something that is out of place with you. Picking up constitutes the largest part of keeping up a house.

Wife: should always run water over dirty pans the minute they are empty. Makes washing them later so much easier.

Wife: should try to keep pans washed up and ingredients used put away before the meal. The after-meal job, when you are tired, won't seem nearly so big.

Everyone: should carry his dishes to the sink and run water over them after each meal. Makes them easy to wash and saves Mom lots of trips.

Wife: should do the kitchen as soon after meals as children's needs allow. Dirty kitchens are depressing.

Husband: should help with dishes whenever possible.

Wife: should get the clothes washing first thing in the morning. Fold or hang them as soon as they finish drying. This, as well as putting fabric softener in the rinse will help keep ironing to a minimum.

Husband: Should allow her to purchase or replace items that need ironing with items made of no-iron materials.

Husband: can make it an automatic two-minute job each morning helping wife spread up bed upon arising. It gets a good start on the day and is so encouraging to her.

Husband and wife: encourage your children to make their beds immediately upon arising, even if they can't do them well. Later they'll be able to. Messy beds are depressing.

Husband and wife: teach the children to pick up their own toys several times a day and put them away. Later on, they'll love neatness (hopefully).

Wife: should set a goal timewise for cleaning each room. For instance: 10:00-10:30, the bathrooms. 10:30-11:00, family room. She can't always reach the goal but it will help.

Wife: should get 15-foot cords on the telephones so she can quietly clean the kitchen, straighten drawers or other chores while talking. The technique is not hard to master and saves hours. Of course, conversations that require deep concentration are exceptions.

Wife: should work as fast as she can at unpleasant jobs, and tackle them first. Leaving them until she is tired almost assures their not getting done or done right.

Husband: never, never leave anything for her to pick up: clothes, shoes, hobbies, magazines. She isn't your mother, or your servant.

Husband and wife: finish one job before starting another, if possible. If not, put the first job away and take it out another day. One never seems to "get back to it" as planned.

Husband: when things start getting ahead of her, grab the vacuum cleaner. Or do the windows. Or mop and wax.

Wife: Keep a list of needs and shop in volume. Frequent trips to the store play havoc on organization. Going there without a list is a real time-waster.

Everyone: Unpack suitcases immediately upon arriving home after a trip. There will be enough messes to clean the next day without adding that one.

Husband and wife: Clean up party messes after guests have gone, no matter how late it is. You'll be glad you did the next morning.

Chart the Day

My husband accomplishes more in any given period of time than anyone I know. He is a list maker. He maintains two: one for the office and one for home. He crosses off the tasks as he accomplishes them. Those that remain undone at the end of the day go on the next day's list. Each day he tries to work on something big on his list that can't be done in one try. His temperament and abilities work together to make him a perfect list maker. It comes naturally for him. But for me, it doesn't. It is very difficult for me to fit into any mold, and self-discipline does not come naturally. But through the years, seeing the tremendous help it has been to him and to our family, and because he has wanted me to, I have attempted to put this method to work in my own life as well. I'm still very faulty with the system, but what I have learned to utilize has helped me immensely.

Taking care of a family doesn't always fit into a schedule, and no home can be run like an office, but charting the day to allow for housework, playing with the children, napping, creating, cooking and preparing for husband's homecoming will keep the time from flying away with little accomplished.

Get Outside Help

The house should be thoroughly cleaned at least once or twice a year. If you can't afford to get a cleaning woman in for three or four days then, husband, you can set aside a few Saturdays to be the outside help!

It's a time of cleaning every cupboard inside and out, debugging the house, removing wax from the floors and redoing them, cleaning walls and woodwork, touching up chipped paint, cleaning windows and screens, doing an extra job on the furniture, cleaning the corners and throwing away old things. The garage and the outside can be part of this. It will make your wife's housecleaning much, much easier in the ensuing year, and she'll never forget the fact that you cared enough about her job to help her with it.

Keep Repairs and Yard Up

A man who can't stop a leak, or despider a house, or fix a piece of broken furniture is one who is at a great disadvantage financially, and if the jobs are ignored, he is at a disadvantage as far as his relationship with his family is concerned. His boys grow up to be the same way, frustrating more wives who have to wrestle with the problems. You may not be a super carpenter or plumber, but you can learn to do most jobs.

Your wife will be able to keep your house much neater if you build adequate space for her. One reason big houses look so much neater sometimes is because there is a place for everything.

If your wife receives your help in the house, she will probably be delighted to help you in the garden. It's a fun thing to do together. She shouldn't be relegated that job on top of her other work, however. Nor should she be left out of it. She likes sunshine and puttering, too.

I don't believe there is anything my husband won't tackle and can't do. It stems from two facts: first,

when he was 13, his dad died and he had to become
the man around the house. Then he believes in
the philosophy of the old poem by Edgar Albert
Guest:

> Somebody said that it couldn't be done
> But he with a chuckle replied
> That "maybe it couldn't" but he would be one
> Who wouldn't say so till he'd tried.

You remember that one don't you? It goes on to say:

> So he buckled right in with a trace of a grin
> On his face. If he worried he hid it.
> He started to sing as he tackled the thing
> That couldn't be done, and he did it.
>
> From *Familiar Quotations*

My husband even built a little house in their back-
yard when he was 15, which his folks are still renting
out to others. The money helped him through school
as well as the other children in the family. Of course,
the little house left a lot to be desired. When he had
it almost finished, his mother pointed out that the
kitchen was bigger than the living room, so he had to
adjust that little oversight.

But never mind. If you have two left hands and
three thumbs on the right, you can still learn. It is
very discouraging for a woman to have to put up with
a house that is only working halfway. I seldom ever
mention anything that needs doing to George. I don't
have to. Each Saturday he and Vance make the
rounds to discover what needs repairing, put them
on their list, and do them as quickly as they can.

She Needs a Full Eight

Make sure your wife gets her proper rest. If she
gets to bed at midnight and the children awaken her
at 6:00, she's going to be too tired to do a good job

with the house or anything else. Keep that in mind, too, when you want to make love.

If you snore, and it keeps her awake part of the night, perhaps she can slip away to another bed somewhere in the house several nights a week so she can sleep soundly. Your attitude on this is most important, for if you are going to be upset about it, and read something into it that isn't there, she'll continue being tired and feeling guilty if she attempts to correct the situation. Of course, it would be wise for you both to cuddle before she leaves, and it shouldn't interfere with your lovemaking.

Sweet Tooth!

Encourage her to cut down on sweets and stimulants. Both items give a lift shortly after consumption, but soon after there is a drop in the blood sugar, as we mentioned in Chapter Five. Another cup of coffee or a roll to "perk up" the body causes the circle to be repeated until finally, after some years, the organs of the body stop responding out of pure exhaustion. You have a weary wife most of the time, and she is ripe for illness. The problem may be yours, as well. A fresh peach or orange break makes much more sense, since sugar in its natural form raises the blood sugar but not to such a dangerous extent. Besides, it will help her weight problem, if she has one.

Good Health Is Worth Working For

Start reading up on the latest interest in health foods and vitamins. Many doctors are changing their whole method of medical practice, or adding to their present knowledge, treating diseases and fatigue with diet and vitamins. One doctor told me, "I believe in a few years we will see the medical profession moving in this direction as a whole." Visit the health food stores and browse through their books. Avoid the "way out" stuff. There's plenty there that makes good common sense. One member of your family may not need anything different, but another, whose body is not able to handle sickness as well, may need a lot different approach to health.

Some authorities believe heart attacks and other illnesses that affect husbands begin in the kitchen with the loving hands of the little wife who unwittingly tears the body down with the materials she uses in her food preparation which she learned from her mother who was taught by *her* mother. It behooves one to find out.

Machines to the Rescue!

If you are a young couple, you should seriously set about obtaining a dishwasher, an automatic clothes washer and a dryer as well as a vacuum cleaner. Smaller helpers such as a blender and electric mixer run a close second. A man who buys a set of golf clubs or the latest fishing equipment while his wife is still struggling through the horse and buggy days in her household, is asking for lots of trouble in his marriage. She simply will not be able to cope with it.

One time during the remodeling of our kitchen (which my husband was doing), I was without a dishwasher for several months. I was astounded to find that I was spending up to two additional hours a day in the kitchen because of it. What a relief it was when the dishwasher was finally put in its place.

Trips down to the laundromat when you need your clothes washed, especially if you have a baby or children, is rather like the person who rents a house instead of buying. His money is going into someone else's pocket and he's no further ahead as the years go by. Also the time spent going to the laundromat and the money used for gasoline and car upkeep mounts up.

Compliment Her!

If she cleans the family room today, make a sweet fuss about it. You might even use my husband's approach. Or you can clean just *one* of the other rooms, saying, "The family room looks so nice, I'm going to make this one equal it. Besides, it'll help you out." Then help her maintain those two clean rooms for a week or so by quietly picking up and straightening. That will encourage her to do a third room to match! Gradually, as she sees your pleasure and hears you say, "I'd be proud to have someone drop in right now, it's so clean," she'll want the entire house to follow suit.

If you never make it known, in a nice way, of course, that you prefer a neat house, she may never try to improve.

Push Her

Some people tend to be on the lazy side by natural temperament. One friend told me, "I have to be pushed. I just don't have a self-starter." But once she gets going, although she isn't fast, she's thorough and efficient. If your wife is like this, you will have to set definite time limits for her in which to get things done and have a sense of humor when she doesn't quite make it. Be gentle and kind, remembering all the other lovely things about her that we pushers and rushers don't have . . . like her calmness, for instance.

*

P.S. Uh, uh, wife. No place for self-pity here. Or martyrdom. If husband is slow to come around in this area, redo your own approach, no matter if he understands your problems or not. You're a big girl, now. Some things you may have to gently insist on, in order to be lovely, healthy and appealing to him as the years go by and to be a good mother to your children.

8

Exciting New Wife

Eeeeek!

The anguished screech didn't come because the little woman saw a mouse, but because she saw five additional pounds registered on her scales. Our survey revealed that all but one woman felt she was overweight. To you, she may be just right. You may not even notice what she considers plumpness. She feels just as good as ever in your arms. In fact, you may like a little more flesh than some. Tell her over and over again.

But if she is concerned, and *feels* overweight, and if she isn't as lovely as she thinks she should be, she might not look as lovely as she could. That extra sparkle might not be there. You, the strong one, can help her, and if the problem is yours as well, you can help yourself at the same time. If she is overweight and doesn't care, but you do, don't despair. Maybe one of the following suggestions would be your ticket to a slimmer, happier wife.

. . . . Encourage her to go to a reputable salon. The exercises are great, too. She can share what she learns with you.

. . . . Be willing to go without fattening desserts and large helpings of starchy foods. One can get used to fresh fruit and even prefer it once the pattern is set.

. . . . Hold out a beautiful reward: $1 for every pound lost; a cruise on a ship; a new outfit; a weekend honeymoon; $100 to do with as she pleases. Cut out a picture of the reward and paste it on a refrigerator (nothing negative, please).

. . . . Put her under competent medical care.

Your Hair Looks Beautiful

Do you feel impelled to say that to your wife very often? If you haven't noticed lately, or if you find your head turning when a lovely head of hair on another woman floats by, take a good look at your sweetheart. If her hair is short and you prefer long, ask her to do something for you that will make you very happy—let it grow. She can still put it up in back for the short look when she prefers. If her hair is too thin to look good long, suggest that she get a little hairpiece to fill it out. If your wife never changes her hair style and you wish she would, point out hairdos you like and suggest, "Honey, fix your hair like that one of these days soon, will you?" If she retorts,

"What's wrong with mine?" you can say, "Oh, yours is lovely, but variety is nice, too." If she does attempt new hairdos and they don't come out too well at first, don't laugh, encourage!

If she is graying, she can get a rinse to give her hair new life. The emphasis is on youth in our country, and many a woman, who was unable previously to land a job was able to do so once she colored her hair.

A full wig for special occasions is a wonderful boost for a woman who wonders if she can compete with the other women who will be at the office banquet. Wigs are less expensive in the long run than a weekly trip to the beauty parlor anyway. They only have to be fixed professionally once in awhile. And they provide variety for her and you. Some synthetic ones look just fine. Others look very cheap. She should buy carefully. Real hair wigs are usually very good although they cost a bit more.

Some men blow sky-high when they come home to find their wives have new cuts or hair styles. They poke fun at the lady who is attempting to look as attractive to her husband as the girls in his office. I'm sure you would never be so unkind. If you come home to find your wife looking different, she will feel foolish until she has your assurance that you think she looks lovely. If she really doesn't look lovely (be sure you don't make a hasty judgment), and you don't approve of her new makeup, her false eyelashes or the new wig, wait a bit and then gently tell her that even though she looks okay with her "new equipment," you preferred her without. But be sure. If you say no this first time, it is unlikely she will ever try it again. Give it a week or two before deciding. If she has cut her hair and you don't like it, remember hair does grow out and can be restyled. If you insist your wife look the same year in and year out, however, she is likely to tire of herself and feel like an old comfortable hat, and you, without realizing it, may be showing your insecurity.

Clothes Make a Difference

Clothes don't make the man, but they surely can help! The head of a large religious high school always insisted that the football boys wear dress suits when they went out of town to play a game. It was her contention that when they were dressed like gentlemen, they would act like gentlemen.

There is a time for old clothes and the play-on-the-floor-with-the-kids look. There are times when every marriage partner must look rumpled and unkempt. It is unnatural to look like a fashion plate 24 hours a day. When you have to grit your teeth and avert your eyes rather than look at your wife in the morning (if she didn't get up early enough to improve the situation) just remember, that cute little doll at the office doesn't look any better before she leaves for work either. And if you are normal, you probably aren't any prize before breakfast either. But it is true that we feel special when we dress up. Your wife can't feel gorgeous in last year's house dress, husband. That should be relegated to her cleaning times when you aren't around. Basically, her wardrobe should consist of the following:

1. A few "dress-up" clothes for going out to dinner, church or other special places.
2. A few good-looking outfits that she can be wearing when you get home, ranging from cute to provocative. Pants are great, but encourage dresses, too.
3. Housedresses or outfits for working during the day, but which don't make her look like a freak should someone come to the door.
4. Grubbies for real dirty work and play.
5. Some cute play clothes for fun outside with you.

As human beings we tend to follow the crowd so much, or get so comfortable with something that we don't want anything else. One time my husband and I were in Palm Springs after a series of meetings he was attending in Los Angeles. Going out to dinner,

I put on a fancy dress and we started downtown. What should we see walking up and down both sides of the street as far as we could see? Pants! Men's pants and women's pants. It was really very amusing to see once again how, when we are sold on a style or fad, we go all out. It reminded me of a photo I saw of a large mass of young women on a college campus in years gone by. Every one of them looked like she had been stamped out with a cookie cutter—short, cropped hair, calf-length full skirts (gathered) with bundles of big petticoats underneath and almost identical blouses. There is security in wearing what everyone else is wearing, but I personally like to see people be a bit individual.

That wardrobe need not be large, but it does have to be replenished from time to time. The old adage that you should buy as fine a quality as you can afford is probably a good one. In the long run, you pay no more than buying those that fade, shrink or don't wear well. If she has invested in good quality, she will have those to wear along with the new things she gets from time to time. High price does not necessarily indicate quality, of course. Items should be carefully chosen. If she sews well, you are that much further ahead, although she shouldn't be expected to sew everything she wears, unless she insists on it.

If you are a man who believes in buying only enough clothes to cover your indecency, you can't expect your wife to be able to compete with the women you see every day at your work. And if you maintain budget-wrecking recreation, hobbies or habits, but resent buying new clothes for the one who should be the most important person in your life, she will have trouble not resenting the position to which you have relegated her—the last on your list.

Makeup or Not?

It depends. The keynote seems to be, as in most things, moderation. Women, as they grow older sometimes need to enhance their natural beauty more than younger ones who have the beauty of youth on their side. Overdone or poorly applied makeup is no help to anyone, no matter her age.

One boon that is coming to the market is the idea of makeups with vitamins and natural ingredients in them. The skin readily absorbs anything put on it. How much better to furnish it with body builders rather than chemicals that tend to age the skin.

If you tell your wife today that to you she is:

the most beautiful woman in the world, or

the most precious, adorable creature in your life, or

like a pretty flower, or

a living doll or

a sexy woman who turns you on, or

an exquisite treasure, or

anything that makes her feel smashingly attractive in your eyes, the next day she very likely will be puttering around with new makeup, trying new perfume, redoing some old clothes or buying a new item to keep your eyes shining. The cost will be minimal compared to the joy it will bring her when your eyes light up.

If she doesn't respond to your innuendoes the next day, it may be because she's in shock. Try it again, and again, and again, and soon you will see her begin to respond.

Her Talents

I'll never forget the tears I saw in a woman's eyes when she came up to me after I had spoken at a women's luncheon. She had an unusual talent in music and was a concert pianist before she married. Her husband, though he knew this, decided that a woman's place was in the home. He would not allow her to use her piano for anything but her own entertainment. Her abilities were a threat to him. He had never grown up emotionally.

Such an incident parallels sadly with that of a man who has a desire to be a forest ranger, but his wife, preferring the city, threatens him with divorce if he doesn't stay there and work the rest of his life as a store manager. He cannot realize his deepest dreams.

The husband of one young wife who had been used to accompanying musical productions and singers, sold her piano the minute they were married. It meant too much to her, and he couldn't stand the competition. Of course, that marriage was doomed before it began. Some women can be put on a chain which is unlocked at periodic intervals so they can graze a little in a nearby pasture, and they will munch away contentedly all their lives, but more and more such women are trying to pick the lock off to get free, or are out and out bolting.

How much better it would be if they were free to do what they wished in using their talents, but decided to limit themselves because their husbands were so wonderful and fantastic and fulfilled them so completely as women, they didn't have the need or desire to go too far.

Your wife may have lost her desire to "do" things through the years if you have suppressed it, or allowed only certain types of outlets. Generally, most men approve of their wives 1) being in the missionary society or other church activity if it doesn't take up too much time; 2) working at a job where she gets paid; 3) sewing; 4) painting and other art—if it is done at home; 5) writing—if it is done at home and before he gets home from work; 6) singing in the choir and solos in the church; 7) other "safe" activities.

Who's in the Limelight?

Frightening to some, perhaps because of male ego (insecurity), or fear that she will neglect the family and house, or because he wants her at his beck and call are such things as professional performing, public speaking, executive positions, jobs that pay more than his, managing major money matters or anything where she gets the limelight more than he.

A well-known head of state said that nobody could influence him; nobody at all. Certainly not a woman. He said that in a man's life women count only if they are beautiful, graceful and feminine. He charged that women never had in their ranks a Michelangelo or a Bach, or even a great cook, even though women haven't lacked the opportunity to give history a great cook. In his opinion there are and have been no great women—none!

Unlike this monarch, most men recognize that women have made the top in many fields. They also realize that women have not had the opportunity to show what they can do. A great cook? There are many, but their activities have by custom, been confined to the service of their own families.

Without a doubt, in countries where Christianity has made little or no headway, women remain at the foot of the pile, often treated as a piece of property rather than as a human being. Many men quote this as an example of what will happen if women insist on their "rights" as is being done in America today. One journalist pointed with glee to the "liberated" woman of Russia. Her husband does not help her at home and her house labors are done without the time-saving devices American women have, with only one family in ten having a vacuum cleaner, for instance. Women there account for nearly half the work force in industry, yet few will ever see top management positions. They send their children to day nurseries so they can go out to work on the construction gang, building a road. A Soviet woman journalist was quoted in *U.S. News & World Report:* "A girl doesn't realize that the years given over to a 'male' occupation can rob her of the main thing: her happiness as a woman, the joy of motherhood." Now it seems she may have a message for the women in free countries as well.

A man has infinitely more opportunity to pursue a career of his choice than a woman, but that doesn't mean the imbalance is right. God gave women talents and abilities and He intended them to be used. For her to use them in a degrading way is another thing entirely and can destroy a life as easily as not using them at all. But to deny human beings the privilege of developing the gifts that are theirs by nature is cruel indeed. To insist a woman subjugate herself entirely to another's personality is pitiful unless this is her basic desire.

Granted, the natural division of activities is dictated by the fact that women have babies, not men. Girls tend toward domestic activities, even in their play. I was amused to read in a women's freedom magazine a report of a test that was taken in a nursery school. No matter what they did to teach the children differently, when they were left to their own devices, the boys played with cars and the girls went over to the dolls. Then they noted that in the PTA the mothers baked cakes while the fathers made policy. Their conclusion was that this "lie" had to be unlearned. No matter how they might wish it different, it is natural for women to be the homemakers and men to be the providers.

When Adam and Eve were put in the perfect garden as perfect man and woman, no such decision had to be made. The food was there for them to eat as they needed it. The weather was perfect, so there was no home to build or keep, no dishes to do, no clothes to worry about, and had they been blessed with children before their fall they undoubtedly would have joyfully shared the responsibility, even though Eve would have dominated the situation a bit for she would have nursed the babies. But after the fall, food was no longer plentiful. The weather was not ideal. Animals were wild and dangerous. Even though it was part of his punishment to toil for food, it was only natural for Adam, the physically stronger of the two, to battle the forces of nature and "bring home the bacon." Their existence was one of survival. But that isn't the story in modern America!

Most men are willing to put up with the numerous sacrifices necessary if their wives work outside the home as we mentioned before, for it means extra money coming in, and they are being directly benefited by it.

It might be well to look at the results of an interesting study reported from Washington, D.C. It revealed that families in which the wife held down an outside job usually found their bills skyrocketing. Such a wife spends more and lives on a higher plane financially than does her contented stay-at-home sister. Of course, a woman may work because the compensation she receives and the need she fills in her job make her feel appreciated and respected. Since her job as mother, wife and housekeeper may reward her with criticism and lack of appreciation, she chooses the romance of outside employment over the job at home.

Yes, a man often doesn't mind his wife bringing money in from a steady, so-many-hours-a-day job and he is willing to put up with the inconveniences and sacrifices that go with it, but when it comes to hobbies or pursuits that take the wife outside the home for anything extensive, and it isn't bringing money in, he "draws the line." It is a rather sad commentary on what we consider important.

A woman should handle only as much as she is able to handle well. If she is a wife, she has responsibilities toward her husband just because he is another human being, if nothing else. If he has agreed to treat her the way a woman likes to be treated (feeding, housing, protecting and loving her), she should, in all fairness, agree to tend to many of his needs as well. If she has given birth to children, she is denying her very heritage as a woman if she cheats herself out of the exhilarating job of forming those lives. So, as a wife and a mother, she should do the job as well as possible. Some women cannot handle any more than that nor should they be expected to, if they don't want to. However, the average woman can handle diversionary activities and she needs them if she is not to become dull and uninteresting to her husband.

One husband in our survey complained that his wife didn't want to do anything different, and he felt she should. Such a woman may be lazy or insecure. She needs to be built up to believe in herself and her accomplishments and pushed firmly but gently into doing them.

For a man to refuse to make sacrifices to help his wife so she can have diversionary activities, is to be unreasonable and selfish.

The Benefits Are Worth It

A minister told me it took him a long time before he was secure enough to admit he was not letting his wife develop as a person. This revelation came about the time he realized that he was not allowing *himself* to develop either. He kept things to himself, feeling it was manly not to share his innermost feelings. As a result of both points of immaturity, walls began to go up in their marriage and the relationship was not ideal. Since he counseled others, he had to come to grips with this problem and do something about it. He began to realize it isn't at all masculine to be the unapproachable king who holds out the scepter to his Esther so that she might ask his favors. Esther's husband, Xerxes (Ahasuerus) was an ungodly man, and a cruel Persian king. God's man is patient and kind and easy to be entreated. This young pastor unhooked the chain from his wife's life and began to share with her his fears and joys and thoughts. He suggested that she reach out in her own way to fulfill some of her deepest desires. She, with her new-found freedom, scarcely knows which direction to turn. She goes bowling with several other women while Papa baby-sits. She's aglow with the thought that now, at last, she doesn't have to fit into the little mold husband had decided she must fit into. She can decide what she wants to do and pursue it and he will back her all the way. This wise man says it has made all the difference in the world in their marriage. He feels more like a man than ever before, and indeed one who is within the bounds of God's will, not the iron-clad rigidity of the prison he had made for both himself and his wife.

A friend of mine tells that, just before she married, she was very insecure, recovering from the heartbreak of a disappointing romance. She had no idea of her own potential. After her marriage her quiet husband (who had come up the hard way and worked at many occupations in order to become the professional man he is now) saw the potential in this woman. Instead of suppressing it, or being afraid of a shattered ego, he encouraged her. He drew her out. He gave her the go ahead and that's what she did. She went ahead like a galloping mare! She teaches gymnastics and leads her class into spiritual truths. She is a real estate agent and when the mood hits her, she sells a house. She's a decorator and when the mood hits her, she does it professionally. She has a pilot's license. She has been a sales woman and a whirlwind political campaigner. Her life is a constant whirl. I never know what she has been doing when I talk with her. Her house, very beautiful and very expensive, is always spotless and she does most of the work on it herself. Her family is well fed for she enjoys being a gourmet cook. Never have her activities been a source of trouble. Her husband is not only mature emotionally, but he recognizes that he is the one who benefits from her abilities.

My husband's mother was a creative individual, and even in the midst of hardship as a widow with three children, and working at anything she could to make ends meet, she took time every day to work on her painting, her extraordinary photo taking and to write poetry. If she couldn't do it during the day, she would stay up through the night! George learned early that a woman who can occupy herself part of each day with some lovely, creative thing she hungers for, is a happy woman and everyone around her benefits far more than if she is kept on a leash to scrub and grub.

So when we were married, he eagerly encouraged me in my singing, acting and writing. He feels that when I am creating, whether it be in concerts or radio or directing a play, I am an exciting person. He enjoys the results immensely. This is a no all-take and no-give husband. He makes sacrifices so I can pursue these activities, just as I make sacrifices for him so he can pursue his work as an attorney and all the peripheral activities that go with it. He has his own form of creative endeavor, as well.

I have often been amused by those who are worried that I neglect my family and husband to do these things. Some have even hinted that if I'm not careful, I might lose him! What they don't know is were it not for my husband pushing me, I would have quit these activities long ago and settled down as housewife and mother, period. It has taken years of his encouragement to convince me I have something to offer and have a right to offer it.

One morning after church, a man informed me that I was neglecting my children and my husband and needed to settle down to spend more time with them. To him, I suppose, I appeared as a woman who was never home, running hither and yon, leaving my children to cook for themselves, never playing with them, forcing my husband to grab his food in restaurants, leaving the sink piled high with dirty dishes, leaving unmade beds, etc. To him, I couldn't possibly be doing all the things I do and be a good wife and mother at the same time.

If yours is a creative wife and you are fearful she might not keep her priorities straight, perhaps it will ease your mind if I emphasize my conviction that there is a need to do so.

When the children were little, I practiced my singing and wrote my songs while they played in their playpens beside me. Both grew up warbling scales like Mommy. Now, I practice while they are at school or at night when they are in bed, for my husband has always urged me to keep my voice warmed up, even as we traveled in our car. He acts as though even my exercises are beautiful to him so the children react the same way.

Life As Usual

I've always felt it important to start my family out in the morning with a big hot breakfast and a lunch under their arms. And I do not feel there is any excuse for meals of the frozen or canned varieties, except on "emergency" occasions. Our bodies cannot be strong and healthy unless food is prepared properly. I want to give my family the best help physically that I can.

With only occasional exceptions, I am home when the children get here from school. I spend the first hour of their homecoming listening to their tales of the day and helping them plan the rest of the day. All evening I try to be available to them when they need me. Often evening concerts are planned so that my children can perform with me if they wish and my husband frequently goes along to arrange my affairs and set up my equipment. A fine speaker himself, he understands the boost it gives me.

My time to do housework, plan dinner and begin

my creative projects is after the family leaves in the morning. Some days I just clean to get caught up with the big jobs. Other days, I don't touch my housework but dive into a project that has a deadline on it. Those days, I clean after the children come home, while they are doing their homework. Since our house is large, and our family loves many activities, everyone helps me quite a lot, especially on weekends, although I keep up the basic work. When one is available, I try to get a housekeeper, but am without one most of the time.

At my husband's insistence, while working on a project with a deadline or that needs intense concentration, I don't answer my phone. This may lead people to believe I am never home. George feels if it is important, they can always call his office, for he has a code call by which he reaches me. Besides, I'm available after the children come home.

The only time my husband says no to my tackling a creative project that is to my liking, is when he is afraid I am doing too much for my own good health. I never argue with his decisions for he is so mature and wise and he has never been wrong. Yes, it takes a mature man to allow his wife to do more than live in his shadow all her life. Mature men are happier people by far, and the type of women they produce feel no need to walk the streets and wave signs, demanding their rights. They've already got them!

*

P.S. to the husband's personal doll: get going on your hairdo's and makeup, huh? And your clothes; lingerie with holes in it may fool your neighbors, but it won't fool your husband. Keep yourself alluring. And remember—a woman with no interests in life but her children and home has to work harder to be fascinating than the one who is busy about the business of fulfilling some of her dreams. Besides, you'll have to guard against being the meddling mother-in-law once your children leave home if you haven't other fun things to do with your life. If you are one of those who is raring to go as soon as hubby unlocks the chain, take it easy. No woman is successful if she fails the most precious possessions in her life—her husband and her children.

9

Little Kid Stuff

"When I was a child, I spoke as a child, I understood as a child, I thought as a child; but when I became a man, I put away childish things."

1 Corinthians 13:11

An immature wife is a sight to behold. She cries to get her way. She pouts when you offend her. She clams up and won't speak when she is angry with you. She bangs pots and pans when she is upset. She sighs in exasperation if you ask her to do something. She may run off to get an "office" job because she can't accept the responsibility of rearing her own children. Sometimes she nips at the bottle or indulges in food. You know the kind. Perhaps you live with one. She needs to grow up. Unfortunately, her immaturity will not allow the instruction and help that could aid her in becoming a woman. However, if she is intelligent, and has a sincere desire to make the marriage go, she isn't a hopeless case.

One of the most effective ways to get your wife to grow up is to be really mature yourself. If you have a mature wife, it is essential that you be mature if you want her fullest respect. Most men consider themselves very mature, but most women agree that it is easy to spot an immature man, no matter how venerated a position he holds. The immature man is usually the last to know it, and tends to rationalize everything he does that makes him so. In order to sort fiction from fact, let's take a look at some old wives' tales, or perhaps it might be wiser to call them old husbands' tales. They stem from people who act immature but don't want to believe it or change.

"That's the Way I Am and Nothing Can Be Done About It."

That's the way you are—true. Nothing can be done about it—false. What we are really saying is, "I don't *want* anything to be done about it." The term *"prima donna"* originally was meant to indicate the female lead in a production, such as an opera. She was the star. But prima donnas often felt it so necessary to pout and yell and cry to get their way with conductors, managers and people in general that the word has come to apply to anyone who insists upon his or her own way in an emotional outburst. Or, instead of overt expression, the prima donna may be one who quietly insists that things go his or her way, or else, and he closes his ears to all alternatives. These people don't want to change, because change means sacrifice and that's "not my cup of tea, brother." Of course, if you are like that, you will have no desire to put forth the effort to help your wife in the right way. You'll continue to bully, or demand or fight to try to keep things running smoothly. You may even find some measure of success, especially if she is a timid soul, but the price you are paying is dear. If there's any doubt, get a copy of *None of These Diseases* by S. I. McMillen, M.D. and find out what anger, criticism and other emotions can do to your health. The body is not meant to keep up with excesses. It wears out. So, do yourself a big favor! Let yourself become a new man with ideas! That spells STRENGTH, any way you look at it.

"Put Her in a Pumpkin Shell and There He'll Keep Her Very Well."

"My wife's job is to take care of me first, the children second, and the home next, period." The idea *is* reasonable. If you are earning the money, and she is enjoying the benefits, the least she can do is make sure you are fed with delicious, nutritious meals and the children are reared responsibly. You have a right to expect a reasonably neat, clean home, as well. However, if "taking care of you" means she must fit this role seven days a week, dancing attendance on you and the children to the detriment of her own needs and desires, then the idea is not reasonable. Remember, you have a union to go to bat for you when you are abused at work, or you have the joy of being a "professional" and running things your way. She needs a measure of relief too, as we already mentioned in Chapter Seven. If she works an eight-hour-day outside the home, the mature husband will not expect her to do the cooking, cleaning and waiting on. He will share all home responsibilities equally.

"The Wife Shouldn't Make As Much or More Money Than Her Husband."

I suspect the same men who say this would also say it about Blacks and Chicano's, because somewhere in the back of the recesses of the gray matter is the belief that all such groups are inferior to the white male. Prejudice is insidious. We all have it about something at some time, but when it is directed against another person, especially a mate, it needs to be dealt with.

Insecurity rears its head in many ways and in men this is one of the most obvious. Your wife's ability to make more money than you (although the probability is not very likely) is not necessarily because she is superior to you but because the circumstances lend themselves to such a situation. The reverse is true as well. Your ability to make more money than she, is not necessarily because you are superior in mental or physical ability to her, but because the circumstances have dictated the fact.

As we have mentioned before, women have not been encouraged to get into the "big" professions. In most cases, they have not been able to break through the male "caucus" to better positions. Until recently, such a thing was unheard of. And yet many women who have no children at home, or who have to make a living to support a family, have much to offer. It is talent going to waste. I much prefer my husband in the typical role of the top money maker. I have no desire to "prove" myself that way. But should I find myself in a position where I had to take over, because of his death, I would find it a hard pill to swallow if I were kept out of jobs I am able to do well just because I am a female.

If your wife is able to earn a great deal and yet not be cheated out of the joys of being a successful wife and mother, why not? You would be doing yourself a big favor.

"No, Ma'am, I'll Handle the Money Around Here."

Problems over money result in many quarrels in marriage. This is one area where you should be brutally honest with yourself. Are you really better equipped to handle the money than your wife?

One wife told me, "My husband doesn't believe in saving for the future. He spends the money as it comes in, and I can't put anything away. Yet, he feels he is head of the household and therefore I have no right to say anything about the way he spends our money. He feels he will lose his headship if he lets me have any say in it." Here's a man with a very capable and quite brilliant wife. He believes, as he told me in confidence, that to maintain his position as head of the wife, he has to treat her like a child, not an equal. I fear he will be in the same position financially when he is 65 as he is now. He refuses to recognize the strengths of his wife and let her take over where he is weak. He is hurting himself, as well as her, of course, and perhaps even their three children when they will need money later for education.

It is only an insecure or misinformed man who believes it would be a loss of manliness if he let his wife handle the money affairs. He needs to take a hard look at the wonderful gifts and strengths that are *his* and concentrate on those.

It might be well to take a quick check to see if you are really the best one suited to handle your family's money. Ask yourself these questions:

1. When I get a little extra money, do I rush right out to buy something?
2. Do I put away a substantial amount of money every month to save for the future? Do I put *any* amount away?
3. Can I account for where all my money goes each month?

4. Do I tend to play the role of "big spender" when I'm with others?

5. Do I tend to buy nonessentials like new cars, boats or spend money on some expensive hobby when we need items such as a washing machine or need to save for a house?

6. Do I try to get by without medical and life insurance?

7. Do I feel it is important to keep up a classy wardrobe or nice furniture when I have bills outstanding?

8. Do I have a definite budget for our spending and stick to it?

9. Do I "charge" a lot of things?

10. Do I live within our income, not trying to live on a level of those who make much more than I?

If you answered "yes" to numbers 1, 4, 5, 6, 7 and 9 or "no" to 2, 3, 8 or 10, you are not a good prospect for handling your family income. There is a possibility that your wife would be better suited for the position. Or if she has the same problems and weaknesses, you had better sit down together and work out a budget, encouraging each other to stick to it, no matter what, making allowances for the past (due bills), the present and the future (in case the husband dies).

Being the one to handle your money says nothing about your manliness. And if you are poor at the job, it says a great deal about your lack of manliness. Perhaps you don't know how to become a good money manager. Then get professional advice and follow it.

There's More to Be said

Numerous women expressed concern because their husbands have little idea how much prices have skyrocketed yet are keeping them on the same budget they have had for the past ten years. Go shopping with her for food this week, when she's getting a big load, and you pay the bill. You might be astounded at the cost. Her clothes prices have almost doubled, and they aren't made to last like yours, so before you denounce her as irresponsible or a poor manager of the money you dole out to her, give her a chance to explain what her problem is.

Her Own Bank Account?

No woman enjoys being a puppet on a string, or in the position of a child holding her hand out for a few pennies to buy an ice cream cone. Some men cannot begin to know the satisfaction and pleasure it gives a wife to be able to drop into a lovely little restaurant for lunch sometime when she is shopping and not have to account for the money she spent. She gets tremendous pleasure in being able to buy her husband's gifts without having to ask him for the money. She might even wish to splurge on a piece of jewelry someday and not feel guilty about it.

So what's the solution? Many women cannot seem to balance a checkbook. In fact most women I know aren't very good at that sort of thing. But that has little to do with *how* she spends her money. She may be very conservative whereas her husband finds that money burns a hole in his pocket. Yet, she may not be able to keep her account straight while he can. The idea of giving a wife her own little banking account would send many husbands right through the roof.

One attorney, when working with marriage reconciliations, always makes the suggestion that, from then on, the wife be given 1) a household account of her own. Whether large or small, the husband is to stay out of it. Their budget should always be sufficient to handle her affairs with some left over to spend as she pleases; and 2) a savings account of her own which she can use for anything she wishes. This gives her a feeling of independence which is healthy and essential to a woman's sense of well being. She needs to feel her own worth and not like she's on the end of a puppet's strings. I consider this vitally important, after talking with numerous women. It is an awful feeling to be "begging" for money all the time. After all, half of what you make is considered hers by rights, anyway, in many states. Why should she have to beg for the portion she needs to run things? Furthermore, it would make her work at home seem more worthwhile, if she were allowed to salt a little away in a special account for the wardrobe she is going to buy someday when you two get enough money to go on that ocean cruise you have been dreaming of.

Here's An Eye-Opener

I know of two women whose wise husbands saw their potential, placed money in their hands to do with as they pleased, and saw their personal fortunes skyrocket into the millions. Are they proud of their wives? You can bet on it. And they are justifiably proud of themselves for not feeling threatened by their wives' talents.

I find it fascinating to read that Jesus' material needs while He walked the earth were supplied by Joanna, the wife of Chuzas (Herod's steward), Susanna, and many others who "ministered unto him of their substance." He felt women could be trusted with the handling of money.

Marriage Is a Fifty-Fifty Proposition

"If she does the things I want, then I will do the things she wants." Sounds good, but it isn't the ideal.

There is only one way to get your wife to be the kind of person you really want, and that is to think of marriage as being one hundred percent give—and you being the giver. If you approach it this way, her female nature will soon have her giving back a hundredfold until you are overflowing.

"My Wife Is My Property."

Not true. No person should own another person. Slave owners act totally out of the will of God and betray the decency of man. A wife is someone you vowed to live with all your life, to love, cherish and provide for. She is not your property as your dog or cow or house is. She is an individual person.

"When I Make a Statement My Wife Shouldn't Challenge It."

What? Is she an imbecile? Can she have no ideas or opinions of her own? Bruce Larson wrote, "The home is the place where Christ can speak most clearly. I would rather hear God speak through almost anyone else than through my wife or my children. I can take it when He speaks through a minister, or through a friend, or through a book, or through His Word. But to recognize God speaking through my wife's loving rebuke or suggestion takes a great deal more grace. And if God is to speak clearly, whom can He better use than the one who sees me most clearly, loves me most unreservedly, and understands my needs most deeply?"[6] Even the God of the heavens talks things over with us human beings, including the women. The Bible says, "Come now, and let us reason together, saith the Lord." Do we not have the right to entreat the Heavenly Father, over and over again? If the Great King is willing to sit down and talk it over and listen to us, shouldn't the same courtesy be given your wife, especially in light of the fact that God is perfect and you are not? Agreed, she should not challenge you in front of the children, nor should you challenge her for the children to hear. And ideally, her challenge should be as full of love and respect for you as your treatment of her is. A wise and mature man always listens to those around him. If he is truly great, he will be willing to change his mind if he is proved in error.

"My Wife Should Consult Me About All Decisions."

That sort of marriage is not a partnership or even a wife must have been made out of a bone in his foot, rather than his rib. A man who insists on such an arrangement tends to be picky and small. He hasn't learned to delegate responsibility.

"She Had Better Not Keep Me Waiting."

Nearly every man feels it his right to be late home from work, or late for dinner if circumstances dictate, and he doesn't want to be questioned about it. But if he has to wait for his wife to get ready, or at an appointed place where they are to meet, she is usually regarded with heavy disapproval. The husband says in so many words to his wife, "My work and what I have to do is important so you should be willing to wait for me. Yours is not important and so I should not have to wait for you."

My husband usually is a patient waiter, so I try hard to meet his schedules. He learned patience as a child when he had to sit for hours while his mother waited for just the right light to take a picture of a flower or a wild animal in her profession as a photographer. You can be patient, too, if you will always have in your briefcase or pocket a copy of something you have been wanting to read and utilize the time. Horn honking is for the birds.

Her Family Gives Me a Pain

They may give her a pain, too. But these same people produced the person you fell in love with and married. They can't be all bad, and should be treated as warmly and considerately as your own.

"My Wife Should Obey Me Just As the Children Do, and If She Doesn't She Should Be Spanked."

Don't be ridiculous. If you were the vice-president of a company and you failed to do something the president asked you to do, you would think he was dangerously unbalanced if he called you in and tried to spank you. Need I say more?

"The Strong, Silent Type Is Manly."

TV and movies have been the culprits. While many women have thrilled at the John Wayne type who favors his lady by nodding in her direction after ignoring her through most of the movie, I don't know of any woman who enjoys living with that type of man. Suddenly, all the he-man qualities aren't so he-man after all and instead she is saddled with an individual whose life is wrapped around himself and who expects hers to be wrapped around the same idol.

Communication is important. My husband has often said that many couples who come to him for divorce are people who can't talk with each other. Many a psychologist says it is important that people lay aside childish pride and be able to talk. They need to talk about their problems, their joys, their fears. Your wife needs to talk, especially when she has had no one around all day except little people who can barely lisp "three." She needs this communication to be part of YOU. No "woman talk" can take your place.

Where and to whom you talk is important. So, a word of caution! Husbands who exchange guffaws with the men at work over their wives' problems or their intimate relationships are men whose marriages already have termites working at the foundations. And a woman who just has to talk about her husband's faults to the neighbor is foolish indeed. Your lives belong to each other—not to the world. If you have problems, talk with each other about them, or if you can't handle it together, go to a professional counselor or minister. Your wife should be able to tell you if you have bad breath or were wrong in your punishment of a child without your feeling offended. You should be able to tell her that her pies give you indigestion and her hairdos are unbecoming without her becoming offended. But tell each other *kindly* and *lovingly*.

My husband and I discuss everything, if we have time. Some of the most yummy moments in our life together have been when we lay in bed just talking and sometimes dissolving in hilarious laughter over something. I prize the times when I can get him to sit still long enough to give me his opinion about certain matters I wish to talk over with him. The fun part is, I don't have to talk them over with him. He doesn't require that of me. So I want to! Oftentimes he will say, "You decide, honey." Other times he will weigh the possibilities, lay them out for me in his logical, male way, and make his suggestions. When he makes a definite suggestion, I usually take it. If I feel he hasn't considered the whole question, I will push it further, and sometimes he changes his viewpoint. Sometimes, he says a flat NO, when I ask for something (like, "What do you think of my directing the Christmas pageant?") but I never rebel or bolt because whenever he says no, it is for my good.

Once in a great while, he allows me to push him about something he is resisting, like his getting to bed earlier than he had planned because he is exhausted, or calling and writing his relatives. But I never try to run my husband in any way, for he is strong and almost totally self-sufficient. He doesn't need me to tell him what to do and he feels the same about me. Sometimes he will get a call at the office asking if he thinks I would be free to do a concert or give a program. He always answers, "I don't keep her schedule. Call and ask her."

"Women Are Lousy Drivers."

Let's correct that. *Some* women are lousy drivers. So are some men. Classifying all women as lousy drivers is the same as classifying all men as male chauvinist pigs. Such statements are irresponsible. My husband has treated my driving like he does everything else. He praises it. When we go on a long trip, he always has me spell him so he can doze off or rest. A man who insists on doing all the driving when his wife is perfectly capable, is saying to her, "I don't trust you. You can't drive as well as I." Then he loses her respect by nodding along the highway, stuffing himself with stay-awake pills and coffee, rather than using the best source of relief sitting on the seat beside him.

He also is not considerate of the fact that maybe she would like a little variety on a long trip, too. She gets tired of sitting, doing nothing. If there are small children, it is only right that she be relieved of their care. Try sharing the responsibility with your wife. You'll grow to like it.

"Girls Should Be Taught Never to Outdo Boys, Except in Domestic Activities."

Amazing as it seems to some, there are those men who believe that it is a shame to be beaten in a game by a woman. So little girls from 12 years and up are instructed solemnly not to hurt a boy's feelings by winning the tennis match or the race. "They won't like you, and you won't get a husband," they are told.

Of course, there isn't a lot to worry about as far as physical prowess is concerned, because in a few years the boy will pass her up anyway, and she will discover that to try to duck a boy in the swimming pool will only result in a very unpleasant revenge ducking instead.

But the ideas have been planted, not only in the girl's head, but in the boy's. They are taught that it isn't nice for women to beat them—in anything. Some women resent this, and have little use for the breathless, clinging vine who is dishonest in her behavior. A false premise is established by this super-feminine creature and causes much unhappiness after marriage as the girl realizes that she is expected to take second place in everything. Such prejudice prevents some of our brilliant female minds from adding their rich store of talent and abilities to a world run by men and which, admittedly, is falling apart at the seams. To be perfectly fair, one must keep in mind that in some cases, "the hand that rocks the cradle rules the world." Women, as mothers, and as influential wives, must take their share of the blame for the world's problems.

Still, a man who considers it humiliating to be beaten by a woman is a man who is unsure of his masculinity. My husband always considers it something to brag about when I beat him at some game. And now that his daughter is growing up, he has the same reaction to her. If she can beat him at Ping-Pong, he laughs in sincere appreciation. Of course, we are teaching her to take her victories in a feminine way, for anyone who lords it over another, whether male or female, is no prize. If I can do anything better than my husband, he is not only willing to admit it but encourages me. It takes a complete man to be like that. As it is, I consider him far more intelligent and capable than I in most areas.

"We Have a Right to Gossip in Our Own Home."

Gossip is tantamount to criticism. Your children will learn early to view others with suspicion and always see the negative rather than the positive, if gossip is a regular "recreation" at your dinner table. Gossip reduces an otherwise manly man to a simpering old-woman type. I was having lunch one day with a man who is a business associate of my husband's. He told me he can never talk against another person in George's presence. He laughed as he said, "It makes you feel like a fool at first when someone doesn't respond to your gossip and makes it clear he doesn't like it, but I have come to really appreciate your husband for that." He most certainly seems to. He sends many clients to George.

I've experienced the same foolish feeling. I have been all set to share a shocking thing I heard or to speak against someone who "done me wrong," with my husband. I would tell my tale. He would make no comment and his eyes would register blank. Then he would quickly change the subject. I learned long ago that we do not talk against others in our home.

A proverb says, "The words of a talebearer are like wounds, and they go down into the innermost parts. Where there is no talebearer, the strife ceaseth."

"The Wife Should Be the One to Apologize."

Only big men can apologize. It takes a setting aside of childish pride. My husband always apologized even when it was obvious to both of us that it was my fault. It taught me to appreciate his maturity and I learned to follow suit.

If you have offended your wife, or she has offended you, one thing she doesn't wish to hear when you come home is innuendos that make her think you are leading up to satisfying yourself later that night. Most women will respond to a little flower held out to them with a simple, "I'm sorry," or "Forgive me?" Then it should usually be followed up by a good honest talk about why you felt as you did, with ample time and attention given to her to explain why she felt as she did. You may be totally in the right, but a wise person, man or woman, doesn't stand his ground.

Whenever my pride was filling me with indignation, and I refused to talk, George would say, "Now, honey, we can't solve our problem if we don't talk it over. Come on, now, let's figure out how we got into this mess." What can you say to something like that?

"I'm Hilariously Funny. I Make People Happy."

Do you know anyone who is the eternal kid? He loves to couch every compliment in an insult. Somewhere along the line he got the idea that cynicism and backhanded comments were funny or manly. They are neither. They are childish. Such a man may look at a woman and say, "You don't look bad. Not good, but not bad." Or, "She's got lots of brains—feather brains." He can't carry on a conversation with a man, either, without some "clever" insulting comment. He is so pleased with his brand of humor that he fails to notice the glimmer behind the eyeballs of his victim that is saying, "I don't like this guy," even though the smile on the front of the face is polite. He will say, "Well, if my wife can't take teasing, it's just too bad."

There is a harmless kind of teasing that doesn't hurt anyone, and then again a cruel and unkind humor everyone can do without. People like this usually pride themselves on "being able to take it" as well as "being able to dish it out." But the truth is, they find it very hard to "take it" and often consider similar treatment from someone else a direct intent to insult.

One man I know goes into a self-persecution thing whenever anyone offends him, which is quite often. Surprisingly, he never sees how he forces others to the point of aggravation with his backhanded taunts and "funny" remarks. Not very many people like him because of this, and yet he thinks, for some reason, that insulting people is normal behavior.

One time he had teased one of their children until he finally had the younger one in tears. When the child reacted, he sent him to his room, calling him a "big baby." Then he started in on the little woman. "He sure takes after your side of the family, doesn't he? Weak and lily-livered (chuckle)." Then, his dissertation punctuated by laughter, he continued "teasing" about her father and other of her relatives. She smiled wryly, knowing that he didn't really mean it —or did he? Finally, after she had put up with this for nearly half an hour, she turned quietly and said, "With a family like yours, I wouldn't talk." He went into a pout that lasted a week, refusing to speak to her. Since this man is 42 years old, it is doubtful he'll ever grow up.

Once again a proverb: "As a mad man who casteth firebrands, arrows, and death, so is the man that deceiveth his neighbor, and saith, Am not I in sport (teasing or joking)?"

We believe in laughter and fun and lots of it. Every healthy marriage has a lot of laughs in it. Both husband and wife should be able to laugh at themselves while the other members are laughing at them, at least occasionally.

One time I got poison oak all over my face. I looked absolutely deformed! My husband tried not to look at me during the customary ten days it takes for it to go away, but one morning, I waltzed into the kitchen, with my dark glasses on, and announced, "I am Madame X!" George could suppress his humor no longer. He answered with a straight face, "You look like an ex-Madame." We laughed about that many times.

Another time George was stung by a yellow jacket inside his bottom lip. It had swollen terribly, and he looked very much like an underworld criminal or a professional fighter who was given a fat lip by his opponent. I wasn't as contained as my husband was over my poison oak. My laughter began to bubble up from inside. It overflowed and continued for three days, everytime I looked at him. When he laughed in response, it only made him look funnier.

A check list for humor might go something like this:

If it brings a child to tears,
If it causes something sacred to appear common,
If it makes something beautiful look ugly,
If it turns cleanliness into filth,
If it capitalizes on another person's weakness,
If it needs to be off-color to make it funny,
If it causes a heart to ache,
If it brings embarrassment to another,

forget it. It isn't funny.

"Women Probably Should Have a Right to Sexual Freedom, Same As Men."

I submit that neither has that right. But men and women do have a right to CONTINENCE. They have a right to *deny* the *lie*. To teach your son to go out and sow his wild oats is to teach him to reap a lifetime of sorrowful adjustment. The nonthinking statement that he has to do this to "learn" so he will be a good husband is just opposite to truth. He can "learn" with his wife as well as another woman. No wonder so few husbands are able to satisfy their wives. Very often the beginning of the problem was when he took his first pleasure at the expense of a girl who was looking for acceptance. Please don't pass this off because I'm a woman. Men are the ones who taught me this truth!

"I'm Going to Retire."

Good! You deserve it. You've worked hard and now you are going to fish and putter in your garden and write a book. That's great. You won't be as apt to grow old if you keep your ideas young and stay interested in all that is about you. But how about your wife? She's worked hard too, for just as many years. Does that mean she now is to work harder than ever because you are at home needing her attention far more than when you were gone all day at the office? That doesn't sound like a mature man, even if you are 70. You don't want her spending the rest of her life wishing you weren't around! Share all responsibilities with her and free her to do some of her "dream" things as well.

"Tenderness Is Not Manly."

Wrong. We women like some of the little boy we see in our men. It is sweet to us, like you playing with model airplanes, or tossing ball with your son or daughter. We love the way you come to us for comfort when the world has treated you wrong. We love to see your big fingers in a tender act, like wrapping a gift for us, or putting a bandage on your baby's knee. And the tenderness of a rugged man who knows how to make love is a beautiful and thrilling thing indeed.

That kind of "kid stuff" is okay, and part of being a MAN.

●

P.S. to the pretty lady: how about you? Get out the magnifying glass and be honest. Are you still acting like a little girl about some things? Children aren't equipped to face the stresses and strains of life. Nor can they enjoy the fullest depths of joy. It's time to grow up.

10

The Other Women in Your Life

Your woman wants to be the only woman in your life. She wants to think your thoughts are only for her, your desires are only toward her, that you think she is the loveliest of all women and you couldn't live without her. Sometimes her desire to possess you is unreasonable and childish, but a wise man will deal with the other women in his life very carefully.

Your Daughter

Most wives can give way to and encourage a healthy relationship between a man and his daughter. It is normal and right that you and your little one have time together to play, to talk and to get to know one another.

Your daughter needs your discipline. A man who gives firm, loving discipline to his daughter will see her become a much happier woman when she is grown than if he does not. Some psychologists point out that even the daughter's future sexual happiness depends on whether or not her father was lovingly firm with her. A wishy-washy father who can be wrapped continually around his daughter's finger may be rewarded with lots of hugs and kisses in the growing-up period, but is a detriment to her in the long run. Unfortunately, many fathers leave not only the disciplining of the daughter up to the mother, but the companionship as well.

In interviewing one counselor in a large junior high and high school, I was surprised to learn that most girls in this age group who became rebellious and hard to manage were usually found merely to be vying for Dad's attention. As soon as the father realized this in each case, and took steps to correct the situation, the trouble quieted down.

Your daughter needs an occasional luncheon and dinner date alone with her father. She needs to hammer nails with you, or take a long walk without the competition of others for your attention. She wants to race you down the road all alone and have you attend her recital. She needs a special little gift some days just like Mom does. She's becoming a woman and is reaching out for what is hers by rights from the one special man in her life—YOU. Later on, if her relationship with you is healthy, she will transfer that need to her husband.

If she is married, she still needs you, but it is definitely time to cut the umbilical cord. Too-frequent visits back and forth should be discouraged, so she can develop a dependency on her husband rather than you. Their financial problems should remain just that—theirs—without interferences from Big Daddy. No matter how much they may want to take the easy way out with Daddy's money, they are far better off if they handle their own affairs. They have the same right to develop strength and character as you had when you were just beginning. Setbacks and struggles will bring them even closer together if the rest of their relationship is right. You can't buy their love or respect, either, and the more you try the less successful you will be. Your son-in-law needs to become his own man.

Your Mother

Up in the top three as far as importance is your mother. She will always be your mother until the day of her death and she is due respect and honor for that reason as well as others until she leaves the earth. This is a difficult situation for some men to handle, for wives tend to be resentful of a mother's influence in her husband's life, and a mother finds it difficult to give up the one she has nourished, cared for, and formed, to the possessiveness of a young woman.

A man's loyalty and where it should be placed is quite clear, however. His first loyalty is to his wife. You have left your father and mother and taken someone to be with you to share your fortunes or losses, your sickness or health, your joys and your sorrows. If your union with her is good, you and your wife will share a oneness and total togetherness that is impossible between mother and son. The relationship between a mother and her son, at the time of the son's marriage, must lose its former intimacy. She becomes more like the master teacher who has done her job to the best of her ability and now watches from the sidelines as her pupil adjusts to his own way of living with her teaching as his guidelines.

But the relationship does not end and deserves special consideration. Probably no one will ever love you as much as your mother unless it is your father. For that matter, no child can love his parents as much as his parents love him, nor should the parents expect it. But the love between a parent and child is not in the same category as the love between a man and his wife nor should it be compared. What you have to help your mother and your wife understand is that a normal person has many types of love with which he reaches out to others. A person who is possessive and wants to shut out others or who cannot love several people at the same time is emotionally undeveloped. It is an unhealthy way to be and if either your mother or your wife fit into that category, you will have to set certain guidelines which they both understand.

So, even though the wife and her desires should be your first consideration, you do have a responsibility to your mother as well. If she lives at a distance, the one she wants to hear from is YOU, not your wife in place of you. When my husband's mother died, he said, "I'm so glad I never neglected her." And indeed he hadn't. He wrote her every week since the time we were married, and called her long-distance every two months or so. When he was in the Marine Corps, he forgot her birthday one year and, knowing how much she liked to be remembered, and how he had hurt her by not doing it, he promised to write her every day from then on until he got out of the service. He never broke that promise. We discovered a trunk in his old home not too long ago where his mother had kept every one of those letters.

He never failed to send her a little pretty that he picked out himself on Easter, Valentine's Day and Mother's Day as well as birthday and Christmas, and after we were married, he added my mother to his thoughtfulness which thrilled her no end.

Some mothers don't seem to know when they are overstepping their bounds. It is not her place to advise you and your wife on your financial matters, or any part of your home life, including the rearing of your children, unless you specifically request it of her.

Even then, a wise mother will not be quick to advise, but will listen thoughtfully and guide you to think it through yourselves.

My mother once reported to me that George took her aside one day and thanked her for never taking sides or interfering in our life in any way.

One mother who lived at a distance, breezed in after some six years absence and immediately set about making things straight. Her daughter-in-law obviously was not doing things correctly. She promptly began making her son's lunches and babying him as she had when he was smaller. In fact, a lot of the selfishness that characterized his personality from being spoiled, started to grow worse. That son should have set his mother straight from the first day of her visit. Instead he started criticizing his wife and it took some time after the mother had merrily gone on her way, to get the marriage back on a smooth path.

Mothers who "drop in" too often should be corrected, too. She should afford your wife the same consideration she would a neighbor, calling first to see if it is all right, or even better, limiting her "drop-ins" and waiting to be invited. Mothers, especially widows, should be invited for dinner or other family get-togethers only as often as your wife enjoys having her, unless of course she is totally unreasonable about it. If she is, you will have to firmly and lovingly set some guidelines.

Some experts feel it is unwise to use your mother or your wife's mother as a baby-sitter very often. She has a right to her own life and shouldn't feel she has an obligation to help rear a second family. Even if she prefers being an instant sitter, she may become much too dependent on her relationships with you and, even though you are using her as a convenience, in time small resentments may start to mount.

If you have had a good relationship with your mother and your wife does not, it could be you have never given your wife a chance to explain what bothers her. A good talk about it, without anger, might give you a clue as to what to do. There is an old saying: no one knows a woman like another woman. Your wife will tend to see the things in your mother that are not commendable, just as your mother will see things in her that are not commendable. Although your wife should never be encouraged to make a habit of talking against your mother, there should be a time when she can "get it off her chest" and have you a sympathetic listener.

If your mother lives with you, you and your wife have a responsibility to encourage her to be as independent of the family as possible, but to feel that she is wanted and needed. She can have certain tasks that are just hers. One elderly mother cooks dinner each Saturday night. Another has the job of doing the dishes after each meal. She is not a housekeeper that you have hired for her board, however, and it should be kept in mind that her strength isn't what it used to be. She is entitled to an easier life than when she was rearing you. At that time, she did the *bulk* of the work while you did assigned chores. Now the situation is reversed.

Your Mother-in-Law

Pretty or homely, skinny or fat, your mother-in-law needs to be accepted by you. If you are having trouble in this area, perhaps you could remember a few things: 1) Once she was young and lovely like your wife; 2) She may not be appealing now because her husband never met her emotional needs; 3) She was largely responsible for rearing your wife, whom you love.

She may need to be put in her place sometimes, but it would be better if you let your wife do it. It will keep peace in the family. Or if she is the ideal kind of mother-in-law (and most of them are)—never taking sides, not interfering, having her own life, thinking your chilfren are the best behaved children she knows—you should tell her so. Write her a letter or send her a gift. Or should we put it this way? How do you like to have your wife treat *your* mother? Then treat her mother the same way.

Regardless of whether it is your mother or your wife's, research studies reveal that the most successful marriages are those which have the sanction and co-operation of the parents. Their counsel (not meddling) is important and should be considered carefully. The man who gets his ire up because one of the parents makes a suggestion or tries to stop him from making what to them seems like a mistake, is one determined to learn everything the hard way.

Your Sister

What a pity that brothers and sisters often lose all contact with each other. Here is someone you lived with for many years, and although she has her own family as her main interest, no doubt, she would be so grateful if brother would remember her birthday with a card or phone call. It would mean a lot of happiness if she could always count on some remembrance from you at Christmastime. Some families are using cassette tapes which they exchange occasionally to apprise each other of family news. But sisters are like mothers. If they live nearby and take up more of your time than your wife appreciates, it is up to you to set guidelines.

Your Grandmother

If you have living grandparents, they can be a tremendous blessing to your children. To have someone who has given you your heritage, stuck away in a rest home, without visits or mail is a sad commentary on our deteriorating human relationships. Elderly people still have feelings. They hurt deeply. They wish fervently. But when they have lost hope, their lives become a living death. Please don't forget your loved ones who are in institutions or are living alone.

The Other Woman

Let's face facts. Sometime, somewhere you are going to meet someone besides your wife who will cause you to feel a ZING inside. Undoubtedly your wife will have this feeling as well. During a family conference I was privileged to attend at Mount Hermon, California, a noted psychologist stated that married people who say they do not feel an attraction to someone of the opposite sex, besides their mates, at some time or other, are probably not telling the truth. Chemistry is a real thing! If it weren't true, individuals wouldn't be so quick to find other partners after they've lived happily for many years with someone they have loved very dearly.

It Does Happen

Bob loved his wife. Things weren't perfect, and his wife wasn't all he would have liked her to be, but all things being equal, he was reasonably content. The thought of divorce or other women hadn't entered his mind, except fleetingly. The children had reached their teen-age years. Bob was beginning to notice a bit of gray in his hair, his face had wrinkles he hadn't seen before, and he was suddenly faced with the thought that he wasn't that young anymore. He felt as young, but his body told him differently. It was depressing. Just when he was getting well-established financially and leisure time was becoming more possible, he was faced with the truth that age and death weren't all that far off. He was ripe for trouble. And it came in the form of a shapely secretary who had just rid herself of an unhappy marriage. She needed a broad shoulder to cry on. Bob provided that shoulder unwittingly during the morning coffee break. The session wasn't unpleasant. It made him feel manly and the poor little thing did need counsel. The coffee breaks developed into an occasional dinner when both had to work late. And one night it happened. He had touched her hand once too often. Suddenly she was in his arms, and Bob decided this feeling could only mean he was in love. Since it was fresh and new and she was fresh and new, it brought back memories of what he used to feel when he and his wife were young. The whole experience was exhilarating and Bob felt young again! The wrinkles and gray hair took on a new meaning—now they looked exciting, maturely irresistible. He still loved his wife, but it wasn't like this new love.

The Meaning of Love

Bob didn't think it through; nor did he want to. He needed to understand that there are three stages of love. In his book, *Marriage Is For Love*, Richard L. Strauss describes these three stages. The first stage is based on the Greek word *eros*. It embraces sexual love and is concerned basically with physical attraction or any characteristic in another which excites or brings pleasure. It is interested primarily in what it can get. Many marriages that break up do so because *eros* was the basis of the "love" that led to wedding bells and in itself has very little staying power.

The second stage of love is the "friendship" stage or *philia*. *Philia* is on a higher plane than *eros* for it is more concerned about the other person. It is interested in common goals and desires. It believes in the fifty-fifty type of marriage. It too has weaknesses for it can become very self-centered if one side fails to come through with its 50. It cannot stand strain to any extent.

The third stage is *agape* love. This one is the ideal, and the type of love young brides and husbands dream of having. It is an unselfish, giving love with no thought of receiving. It wants only what's right for the other person. It is the type of love married couples could have but seldom do.

Bob, who thought he had fallen in love with the secretary was discovering only *erotic* love again which is seldom lasting. It takes time to develop love based on *philia*, which he undoubtedly already had with his wife, and even more time and maturity to develop *agape* love, which he could have had with his wife if he had been willing to be a mature husband who did everything he could to supply his wife's needs. Had he done so, he would have found his wife an exciting new person and the secretaries would have paled in attraction beside her. He would have realized that *erotic* love compared to *agape* love is like comparing fool's gold to real gold. He could have saved himself, his wife and his children a lot of heartache.

If you are in love with another woman, and your wife doesn't know it, keep it to yourself. If you are wise, you will break off the relationship immediately, realizing that it is based on *eros* and will fade in time anyway. If you rush into divorce and remarriage you may regret it the rest of your life.

Remember, it takes years for a relationship to jell. The priceless memories you and your wife share of baby's first tooth, the first raise you received and your first big vacation would never interest a new woman, especially if she were much younger. She could never be as much a part of you as your present wife, until a number of years had gone by. It would be far wiser to work on the marriage you have with the woman you have.

"And why wilt thou, my son, be ravished with a strange woman, and embrace the bosom of a stranger? For the ways of man are before the eyes of the Lord, and he pondereth all his goings. His own iniquities shall take the wicked himself, and he shall be held with the cords of his sins. He shall die without instruction, and in the greatness of his folly he shall go astray" (Proverbs 5:20-23).

The worst possible thing that can happen to most women is their husband falling in love with another. One young woman I knew left her husband for three weeks to visit relatives 3000 miles away. The husband, in a moment of *erotic* love had an affair with a younger woman while she was gone. When she returned, she was confronted with the dread situation. At that time, she was the lovely attractive mother of three young children. Two years later, I scarcely recognized her. She had dyed her beautiful shining black hair to a dull red, and had lost so much weight that she was bony. She had a hard look that was accentuated by the cigarette which was now a part of her that wasn't before. She and her children had lost faith in their "religion," and although she and her husband never divorced, the marriage was a hollow caricature of what it once was. Your wife can far better stand to lose you in death than in love.

Perhaps you married when she was very young. She hadn't the time to develop poise. As soon as she was married, her life became her children and the four walls of your house. It is no wonder that she isn't the sophisticated, charming, clever woman you see at your place of business. She feels devastated even going to a company party. Your confidence in her and your efforts to help her to become well-read and able to develop herself will correct that eventually.

If you feel a bit shaky when you see your gray hair and wrinkles, remember that your wife feels even shakier about her aging. For no matter how you cut the pie it comes out that you, as an older man, can be attractive to a younger woman. But seldom is an older woman attractive to a younger man, unless she is wealthy. Your wife is painfully aware of that fact and needs your reassurance more and more as the years go by.

Any woman who has to live with the fear that her husband might replace her or share his affections with another woman, will find it difficult to be beautiful and alluring in her mind or his. You might consider what some psychologists and doctors are saying too; that a man searching for pleasure in extramarital sex, is a man who is emotionally still a little boy, unwilling to sacrifice his pleasures for another or to realize his responsibilities.

One salesman said to me, "Few women have any idea what we face out there in the world." Temptations *are* great, especially if you travel a lot. But remember, though temptations may pound on your door, you are the only one who can open the door and let them in.

Women in General

There is a lot of heartache in the world you walk and talk in. Hate abounds. People are quick to get offended should anyone act unpleasant to them, and just as quick to respond unpleasantly. I recall with gratefulness the various men I have met in my life whose whole demeanor was warmth and gentlemanliness. I remember the warm twinkle in the eye, the strength of a firm but gentle taking of my hand (instead of a bone-breaking handshake), or the helping with my chair when my husband was not available. These rare individuals never give you the impression that they are flirting or undressing you mentally. They do give you the feeling that they are sincerely very pleased they could meet you. In an instant, they make a woman feel attractive, interesting and worth their efforts to see that she is treated like a lady.

Most women adore having doors opened for them.

They are terribly flattered when a man jumps up to carry a load for them or stands up when they enter a room. There are men like that around and they spread pleasure among women wherever they go. They are just as considerate of their wives whom they seem to adore. Their wives don't feel threatened with their attentions to other women because they aren't neglected or given reason for concern. They know they have charming husbands and they are proud of them for that reason. These men are of varying ages.

For some years, my radio recording often took me into the late hours. The station was on a dark street that was usually deserted by the time I had to make the dash to my car. I will ever be thankful for a few men there who watched me to be sure I didn't go to my car alone. One was black, another was very young, another older.

You Can Be Charming

I recall a boy of not more than 20 working in the checkstand of a large grocery store. One Sunday morning I stopped after church to pick up a few things and as I went through his line, he looked up from his rush and said quietly and sincerely, "You just look lovely." I glowed all day. We have a man at our church who greets people as they come up the walk. I'm amused to watch the expressions on the faces of wives as he looks at their husbands and says, "I see you brought your daughter with you this morning." Everyone laughs at the silliness of it, but the women are pleased and it starts the morning off just right. You, too, can be charming and spread pleasure wherever you go, with a little effort. Sometimes just a smile or a quiet compliment is all it takes to make some mistreated woman feel it may be worth it after all. She needs you too, sir, even though she has no thoughts of a relationship in mind.

*

P.S. to the wife: wife, you are better for your husband than any other woman could possibly be. Believe that and act accordingly. Prove it by being so lovely his relatives and your children will adore you, not to speak of your husband. Compete with that other woman by becoming interesting, fascinating and irresistible. Make it exciting for your husband to come home.

11

Completely Man!

If you are seriously toying with the idea of launching yourself on a self-improvement program that will turn you into the ideal husband, the every woman's dream, you are well on the way to making your wife the envy of every other wife she knows. One housekeeper I had looked at my husband each time she saw him as if he were the moon and the stars. She said to me one day, "Oh, Mrs. Hardisty, you don't know what a marvelous husband you have. I work in many homes, and those husbands . . . phhht! They are nothing! But yours. Oooooo."

His treatment of me is observed by others. Although his manner is one of reserve toward other women, our home blooms with lovely gifts given him by lady clients of every age who felt that paying their bill wasn't sufficient to express their "thank yous" for his work for them. More than one person has watched our marriage wonderingly. One woman said, "The nicest thing about your relationship is that you seem to be friends. That's what I want in my marriage." Two influential men were visiting in our home from South Africa. There was nothing unusual about George's treatment of me that evening, but these two men confided later to the friend who had brought them that they were amazed at the warmth and love there was between us. They said they were going to change their attitudes toward their wives. They hadn't realized how cold and hard they had been and how, in their desire to be masculine, they had taken their wives for granted, relegating them to a servantlike position. Both bought special gifts to take back with them, the first time they had done so in all their travels.

This unusual husband of mine isn't entirely the way he is by sheer self-will or because he was born "good." When he was much younger, he had a temper that could blow sky-high. He worried a great deal and was very materialistic. I don't mean to imply that now he is perfect, even though he has brought those weaknesses under control. It's just that I think he is an example after which my son can pattern himself. He is a complete man.

It is true that self-improvement played a role in his life, but it wasn't the whole story. Many a man has pulled himself up by his bootstraps and made startling improvements in himself simply because he wanted to. My father smoked everything he could lay his hands on when he was a young and handsome country boy. He was anxious to prove to the world that he was a MAN! But times became hard and he faced up to the fact that cigarettes were costing him money. Money he needed. Cigarettes he could do without. One day, he went out to a field, threw his pack of cigarettes as hard as he could and never touched another one or anything related to it. Now, that's self-improvement!

Under the Surface

Yes, a man can control huge hunks of his life so that he is in charge! He can put spit and polish on the outside and come out looking like yesteryear's Sunday afternoon parade. But if he looks inside, sometimes the picture is a different color from that on his TV screen. Down underneath the muscles and brawn and the newfound determination to change is a "tiger in his tank." He's got it by the tail and he can't let go. Steaming around down there under the surface like a volcano, is anxiety, worry, hatred, impatience, selfishness, greed, little white lies, overindulgence, adultery, cruelty, ad infinitum. Do one or perhaps two of these sound familiar to you?

George and I both had to come to grips with the truth of what we found in our innermost beings. We were respectable, nice people who were hiding some things that weren't so respectable and nice. We had somewhat ignored the teachings about God that we had heard for so long, feeling rather self-righteous when we managed to attend church come a Sunday morning. We could improve ourselves so far and then no further. I think the first time I realized God was not only a real Person but was interested in little old me and in what I did, every moment of every day, I could scarcely take it in. Spiritual truths don't come easy, especially when you want to run your own life your own way. But the truth came and, after the initial shock and the thought, "Why in the world did it take me so long to see it?" I got excited. I read about Jesus who claimed to be the Son of God and yet, by some mysterious way too deep for my reasoning to grasp, God Himself! The Jews understood his position. They demanded that the Romans put Him to death for it!

Proof From the Past!

"For unto us a child is born, unto us a son is given, and the government shall be upon his shoulder; and his name shall be called Wonderful, Counselor, The Mighty God, The Everlasting Father, The Prince of Peace" (Isaiah 9:6).

I had always heard about Jesus being the Prince of Peace. But some of those other Names never occurred to me. The Mighty God? Wow! The Everlasting Father? Double Wow! The old Jewish prophecy held new truth for me.

In the Beginning

"In the beginning was the Word, and the Word was with God and the Word was God . . . All things were made by him, and without him was not anything made that was made" (John 1:1,3).

That verse really excited me. I had heard about Jesus being the Living Word of God whereas the Bible was the written Word. Could it be? I read on and came to another verse:

"And the Word was made flesh, and dwelt among us (and we beheld his glory, the glory as of the only begotten of the Father), full of grace and truth" (John 1:14).

Certainly the "only begotten of the Father" could refer to but one Person. My search took me further.

"But unto the Son he (God) saith, Thy throne, O God, is forever and ever; a scepter of righteousness is the scepter of thy kingdom. Thou hast loved righteousness, and hated iniquity; therefore God, even thy God, hath anointed thee with the oil of gladness above thy fellows. And, Thou, Lord, in the beginning hast laid the foundation of the earth; and the heavens are the works of thine hands" (Hebrews 1:8-10).

There it was again. But how could there be more than one God, and. . . . The questions raced about in my mind but I was beginning to understand a little more about the Trinity, which is not three separate Gods but three embodied in One. That's tough for a finite mind. But then, as a friend pointed out, water can be in three states at the same time and still be water (liquid, gas and ice). The third part of the Trinity is the Holy Spirit.

To think this marvelous Person who could be three Persons at the same time was interested in me. The more I read, the more convinced I became of it. In fact, this great God LOVED! Me!

In fact, this love was shown clearly and emphatically while He walked the earth. Here was Jesus reaching out to people so diseased most of us would turn our heads and pass on the other side. Here was Jesus, in demand by thousands, stopping by the well to speak to a lonely outcast who wanted the living water He had to offer.

Here was One who said, "Come unto me, all ye that labor and are heavy laden, and I will give you rest. Take my yoke upon you, and learn of me; for I am meek and lowly in heart, and ye shall find rest unto your souls. For my yoke is easy, and my burden is light."

That sounded good. I liked the gentleness of that passage. Who could hold anything against someone who said something like that? But the meek and lowly Jesus spoke pretty plainly about some things that weren't so gentle. They were strong and cut to the heart.

"And I give unto them eternal life; and they shall never perish, neither shall any man pluck them out of my hand. My Father, who gave them to me, is greater than all, and no man is able to pluck them out of my Father's hand. I and my Father are one. Then the Jews took up stones again to stone him. Jesus answered them, Many good works have I shown you from my Father; for which of those works do ye stone me? The Jews answered him, saying, "For a good work we stone thee not, but for blasphemy; and because that thou, being a man, makest thyself God."

Indeed, it seemed that Jesus was narrow-minded to say the least, for he shouted to the crowds, "I am the way, the truth, and the life; no man cometh unto the Father, but by me."

Surely one couldn't be that narrow-minded and get away with it. What about the good Mohammedans, and the Hindus? What about the pagans? I studied world religions. George studied under some of the country's foremost teachers of philosophy in some of the finest universities America has to offer. Philosophy and religion came to a dead end. Only the way of Jesus went on, on, on into eternity with the promise of not only a full, thrilling life here on earth but FOREVER—and ever and ever. Burdens lifted. Love. Joy. Peace. No more emptiness. No more restlessness. Purpose for living with real meaning. Dare we believe? It raced through my mind over and over again that if the dozens of Scriptures I researched which claimed that Jesus was really God in the flesh were true, then He had a right to be narrow-minded! He had a right to set the path men must follow. No wonder the Scriptures say that we believe on His Name!

We Surrendered

Actually it all began with both of us long before we knew each other. As a purposeful boy of 12, George went forward in his church to receive Jesus as his Savior. As a trembling girl of 13, attending a humble little church camp, I did the same. I believe in that moment, God heard the cry of two hearts and honored it. But I knew little about a great big beautiful world within a world out there, just waiting to be explored, so I went on my way, seldom attending church, never opening my Bible. George's experience was somewhat the same.

When my husband and I first met, he had just bought a new house as well as a new Lincoln and was having a bar built in his home where he intended to entertain numerous people, including young ladies. As an eligible bachelor and a young attorney, the situation was a perfect setup. But his involvement with me soon put an end to that! In the course of our courtship and ensuing engagement, we made some weighty decisions concerning what type of home we would have for our children and what kind of values we would hold. Like all young couples, ours was going to be a perfect home with two fulfilled people running it. But it didn't take long to find out real life isn't as easy as all that. There were far too many times of quarreling, tears, unhappiness and the usual mountains to climb. Something was wrong. Even with an unusually mature husband handling me, the whole situation was far less ideal than we had hoped.

It was shortly after my silverware-throwing spree, described in Chapter One, that the answer finally came. Our daughter was born and with the birth, there was trouble. We had found out that my blood type was Rh-negative while George's was Rh-positive. Although our first child had been born without incident, this one was in trouble and the doctors knew it by the time she was eight months along. They decided to bring her early. Saturday I entered the hospital. George, who was in the delivery room as he had been with our son, barely saw his newborn daughter. She was whisked out of the room to begin the long process of having new blood put in her body in place of her own. I knew she could die, or even be crippled as a result of the trouble within, but the thought that anything worse could happen did not occur to me. In the material I had read on the subject the third possibility had escaped my attention.

So when the doctor came in two hours later to tell me the blood exchange was completed, I was not ready for what he had to tell me. "The exchange appears to be satisfactory," he said, "I don't see any evidence of brain damage yet. . . ." His voice went on but I heard nothing more.

Brain damage! I stared at him speechless, comprehension slowly dawning. As he walked out, a feeling of weakness came. Depression set in and I began to cry. That night, I couldn't sleep. A radio far across the hospital court seemed to blare at me. I wanted to scream. Each time I walked shakily down the hall to the rest room, I heard a baby screaming with pain. I had no idea it was my baby, protesting the sharp needles that drew blood over and over again from her tiny heels. It was good that I didn't know. In any case, I could find no joy in anything nor could I be comforted. They brought her in once for me to see. She was tinier than any baby I had ever seen. She was yellow and listless. It increased my fears.

Monday morning, the doctor came in again to announce, "Elisa's not doing so well. We're going to have to repeat the blood exchange." He hesitated. "This time she might not make it." I said nothing. I couldn't. The exchange was to be done late that morning. I didn't want to know when. I sat in a chair and looked out the window, exhausted, tears throughout my entire body. First, the picture of a brain damaged child would flash through my mind, torturing me. Then the thought would come that if she died, I would never be able to have another baby for the problem would be compounded. I tried to pray but I knew my prayers weren't going anywhere. I didn't know how to reach God. George had brought my Bible and I thumbed through it numbly, trying to find some comfort. I happened upon a verse that said, ". . . If we ask anything according to his will, he heareth us: and if we know that he hear us, whatsoever we ask, we know that we have the petitions that we desired of him." I stared at it. God wrote it. God promised it. Then it had to be true. It had to! I climbed back into bed, calm at last. I pointed to the verse mentally, and directed my attention upward again. I spoke aloud. "God, you've made a promise here, and because you are God you have to keep it. I know it isn't your will that this little baby be brain damaged and that her brother be without a healthy little sister. So, on the strength of your promise, I *demand* that you answer my prayer: If my baby is going to be brain damaged, I want you to let her die. If she's going to live, I want her to be whole and well." I had spoken very slowly and deliberately, weighing my words carefully.

My prayer was crude and ignorant. But in some mysterious way, it pleased God. I felt as if, in that instant, a bucket of peace was poured through my body. Strength came rushing back. My prayer had been answered and I knew it. Never in my life had I had such an experience! I didn't know what the answer would be, but I knew whatever it was, it would be all right.

The doctor came in, gown and cap still on. The amazing thought struck me that the operation on my little one had been going on right when I was wrestling with the Bible verse and praying. He took his mask off and he was smiling. "Elisa made it through the exchange just fine. And I see no sign of brain damage at all. I'm certain she is going to be all right."

After he was gone and I was alone again, I turned once more to the God who had heard the prayer of a little mother and I said, "Lord, thank you. From now on, you can have me. Everything I am and have: my singing, my acting, my desires. I'm giving them to you."

A New Life

Within a month I was in Christian radio, which was doubly astounding because up until three weeks before that time, I had no idea there was such a thing as Christian radio! Within a year, I had a program of my own. I began to see my inadequacies as a wife and to really appreciate the wonderful way my husband handled me. He, too, gave his life totally to Christ.

What happened then? Lightning? Thunder? Were we zapped into superhuman goody-goodies? Not on your life. But we had promises, God's promises of a full, exciting existence forever in a place where disease, sickness, death and wars aren't heard of. We had God's promises about this life, that He would be standing by, indwelling, helping, guiding, protecting, deciding with us. He has never broken His promises to us.

My husband's surrender brought out the real man in him—the complete man! Over the years, this Power has pruned and trimmed and improved him in such a way that I feel sorry for any woman who doesn't have a husband like mine. Much to our surprise, we came to the conclusion that no one can be a *complete* person until he has given his talents and life back to the One who gave them to him in the first place. Being a Christian doesn't guarantee a man like my husband. Some men receive Christ but refuse the pruning action of the Great Gardener, or resist it, so the forming takes much longer and their wives suffer accordingly. But the first step to final and complete manhood is a personal relationship and walk with the Lord Jesus Christ.

We watched with amazement through the next few years as portions of our lives changed, so imperceptibly at first that we weren't aware at times that the change was taking place until it had. We possessed new desires, new goals, new thoughts. We weren't *trying* to change. We were *being* changed, and the process is still going on. George added a spiritual dimension to his life as did I. That's the source of his power to be the kind of man he needs to be and I need to have him be.

We have learned to go to our Leader when we have problems or heartaches. He hears us out, we hear each other out and a certainty of procedure lights up in our minds. The directions have been given. Have instructions—will travel.

Four Dimensions

We are **PHYSICAL**
We are **MENTAL**
We are **EMOTIONAL**
We are **SPIRITUAL**

Neglect one and you are like a three-legged calf, never quite complete.

You can take the suggestions that are in this book, act on them and become a better husband with a better wife. But if you want the ultimate in marriage, you must begin by turning your life over to the One who had hoped to guide it from the beginning. Jesus said that a man must come to him as a little child—trusting, believing, claiming with explicit faith His promises which are recorded in abundance in the Holy Bible.

If you have never known how to pray and don't know how to begin, but you feel the desire, may I pass on to you what my husband suggests:

. . . Bow your heart before the God of the heavens who has revealed Himself to man through Jesus Christ.

. . . Agree with Him that you are in error; that you are sinful.

. . . Ask Him to forgive you for the sake of Jesus who took your punishment on the cross to buy you back from the enemy, the devil.

. . . Ask Him to come into your heart and life to be
your Supreme Boss and the head of your existence from now on.

The miracle starts to take place immediately. He
enters your body and dwells there. Your name is written in the Book of Life. You become His child, a position you can never lose.

One acquaintance of ours, an announcer for the
same network I work for, had been an alcoholic for
years. When at last, he gave his life to Jesus Christ,
the miracle was so immediate that the next time he
walked by the open door of a bar he got sick and
lost everything in the gutter. It was that way from
then on, until all desire for alcohol was entirely gone.

Another close friend of ours was strung out on
drugs, and everything that generally goes along with
drugs. When his surrender came, the desire was taken
away immediately and the Power has led this young
man back into his former haunts to try to win his
friends to Christ.

A housewife friend of mine, who had exchanged
husbands like she would a new outfit (six), found
her peace and what she was looking for in Jesus, and
is now a happy contented homemaker with two fine
children.

A hitchhiker I picked up, a lovely girl of 16, exchanged her life of drugs, sex and running away for
Jesus. Her grade point average shot up, she held
Bible classes, she told about her experience to friends
and family and now she is happily married to another
Christian, a young man she met in the Christian high
school she attended after her conversion.

It Is Real!

None of these people could change themselves.
They tried too long and too hard. It didn't work. You

may not have any such problems or be enslaved in sin as dramatic as this. Neither was I. Nor was George. But you may have felt an emptiness at times and wondered what life is all about. You may wonder what will happen after the grave. You needn't wonder any longer.

If you have prayed as suggested, you can expect great things to happen in your life. If you let the Lord Jesus Christ reign in your life, there is great adventure ahead for you. You, as His child, now have the right to:

Ask for His guidance in your decisions.
Ask His forgiveness when you sin and get it!
Believe His promise that you have eternal life.
Call upon His power to help you with your problems.
Start reading and meditating on the teachings of the Bible and expect Him to begin to teach you the meaning of them.
Expect His protection.
Expect Him to lead you into exciting service.
Expect Him to begin to strengthen your weaknesses.
Expect Him to help you become the husband you should be.
Expect much more than you can begin to anticipate.

No longer the weak person who must follow the crowd, you now march on with PURPOSE and DETERMINATION. You take your lumps, but He is always there ready to soothe and encourage you. You take your thrills, but they come to you in different ways now, and they are far more exhilarating than any you have ever experienced.

•

P.S. To the lady of the house: your husband will need your encouragement to take this most important step of his life, whether you agree with it or not.

Once a surrender to his Creator comes, he will move very rapidly toward being the kind of husband you would like to have. And if you do likewise, you will find it lots easier sledding in your own life. I know. I've been there.

12

The Ideal Wife

I'm sure you have your idea of what an ideal wife should be. Your choice has been influenced by your mother, other people's mothers, your mother-in-law, your grandmother, your sisters, women you have known, tales you have heard and material you have read. Your ideal may be feminine and fluffy with buttons and bows or she may be the tweedy, sophisticated type. She may be extremely brilliant and creative or plain and practical.

If your wife has taken the step of surrendering to the Lord Jesus Christ, she will be eager to search out His guidelines for her life. She might find them difficult to follow for awhile, but her job will be much easier if you supply her needs as outlined thus far in this book.

Orders From Headquarters

We find the Scriptures rich in treasures concerning the wife's relationship to her husband. Most Christian men can quickly quote certain passages which tend to be favorites and support his position as head of the wife and thus head of the family.

> "Wives, submit yourselves unto your own husbands, as unto the Lord. For the husband is the head of the wife, even as Christ is the head of the church . . . Therefore, as the church is subject unto Christ, so let the wives be to their own husbands in everything."

Another favorite tells young wives to be sober-minded,

> ". . . to love their husbands, to love their children, to be discreet, chaste, keepers at home, good, obedient to their own husbands, that the word of God be not blasphemed."

Another says "The wife hath not power of her own body,

> but the husband. . . ."

How does that sound to you? Strangely out of tune with what is going on in the world today? Women are screaming for freedom, not subjection; for independence, not obedience; careers, not keepers at home; a new morality and equal rights, not to love *only* their own husbands. Some feminists declare that the Bible is their enemy!

Perhaps, if you have been affected by current modern thinking, you may sincerely feel that the biblical view is too restrictive for women. Or you may take the opposite view and say, "If the Bible states it, then it is right and there is no need to go further or say more."

One of the most fascinating things about the Bible is the fact that to study it intelligently, one dare not take a single verse or passage and rest his case on it. He will only show his ignorance should a student of the Holy Book come along. The Bible must be studied in its entirety to get a complete picture of any subject approached within. A Book that has never yet been proved to contain a contradiction or an error (only in translations), the Bible takes the highest of human wisdom coupled with the wisdom of God to present a comprehensive, intriguing whole.

So before we either condemn the aforequoted passages as "too restrictive" or accept them as "the whole truth" we must seek a bit further. And that search takes us right to the end of Proverbs. Chapter 31 outlines *God's ideal wife* in easily understood language.

What a Woman!

Here is a woman, we read in verse 10, who is virtuous and thus so valuable that the exquisiteness of the finest ruby pales in comparison to her. In fact she is so virtuous that her husband knows deep down inside himself that he can trust her explicitly, as we are told in verse 11. "She will do him good and not evil all the days of her life," verse 12 informs us. She is his friend.

On to verses 13 and 14: "She seeketh wool, and flax, and worketh willingly with her hands. She is like the merchants' ships; she bringeth her food from afar." No lazy woman, this. She loves to accomplish. She leaves her home in the hands of her servants, and undoubtedly with others accompanying her, she goes to look for the finest of materials from which she can make cloth. Since travel those days was by horse or some other slow means, I doubt if she was able to dash downtown and be back in two hours. No, her journey to the city where the big markets were may have taken several days. In fact, she may have met the ships when they came in and dickered there for wool, flax, and food.

She was an aggressive woman, was she not? Not crude or loud, for she brought no shame to her husband, but she knew what she needed and moved definitely to get it.

As we have already seen, here was a woman whose husband realized she needed help. His line of work may not have afforded him time to do the labor around home himself, but he didn't need to, for he worked hard enough to hire servants for his busy wife. But even though she had servants, she realized that probably no one could feed her family as well as she, so; "She riseth also while it is yet night, and giveth [food] to her household, and a portion to her maidens." At least she was on hand to be sure the cook served up body-building, nutritious meals, planning her menus while the house was quiet and she could organize her thoughts.

While the servants were doing the scrubbing and cleaning and baby-sitting, she was over at the neighbors or perhaps on another overnight trip to look over some property she had heard about. She walked through the piece of land to determine whether or not it would be profitable. We might be able to assume that the lady had her own tidy amount stuck away in the matza jar. Her husband undoubtedly shared generously with her and besides, she was enterprising enough to have a couple of businesses going on the side. Her affluent husband was a very intelligent man and a shrewd operator. He knew his wife was capable. He also knew that a brainy, clever woman operates best when she doesn't have someone hanging over her, governing her every move. He trusted her to make some mighty big decisions without his having to be the final word. I suspect she talked most matters over with him and got his opinion. When a woman loves and respects her husband, she enjoys doing that. And I suspect his comments went something like: "Well, dear, you saw the property. If you feel it's a good buy, then get it." She didn't need to beg him to take over the job she'd started because his encouragement in the past had caused her to develop her abilities to the point that both could feel confident she would do the right thing on her own.

Fulfillment Assured

In fact, having such a capable woman probably relieved this outstanding man a great deal, for he was able to carry on his career in politics and running the city. "Her husband is known in the gates, when he sitteth among the elders of the land," we are told in verse 23. His success in his chosen career is another indication that he was a mature, wise person who didn't feel it necessary to prove his superiority by bossing his wife around. Can you picture this fantastic man charging into the house, flinging orders at his wife (except in an emergency situation), cranking at her because she isn't doing things "his way" and insisting that she stay in the kitchen to boot? I can't.

But back to the property. "She considereth a field, and buyeth it." Then, "with the fruit of her hands she planteth a vineyard." She dipped into the matza jar again! She tapped her money sources to hire her workers and begin her project. She decided on grapes. The land was good for grapes. So was the climate. Besides, she liked grapes. They were nutritious, providing food and juice for the family. And likely, the rest of the crop was sold because the wine and juice from them brought in even more money which she could tuck away in her stocking because her favorite jar was full.

She was a strong woman, we see in verse 17, not only physically but emotionally as well. Indeed in verse 18 we see: "She perceiveth that her merchandise is good; her [lamp] goeth not out by night." Not only did she work long hours to fill her orders, but when the going got tough, she was a shining light and optimistic strength to those around her. A woman who is constantly fearful of what husband is going to think can never have that sort of strength in its fullness. She knew, because her husband was mature and believed in her, that he would be pleased with any decision she made. He didn't blow his stack when she made a mistake. Had he done so, her emotional nature would have held her back from making further decisions for fear of the volcano.

With all of her journeying to the market, preparing food, dickering, purchasing, planting and tending to her family's needs, she still took time to help the beggars that came by the ranch. No doubt she made a few visits in person to take goods to the widow that Lemuel left behind for, "She stretcheth out her hand to the poor; she reacheth forth her hands to the needy." Once again she made decisions and followed through. Helping the poor was her special service to the Lord.

A woman this well-treated undoubtedly considered herself to be very attractive. Certainly her husband had made it clear that she was to treat herself as a lovely person, for he approved of her beautiful clothing, worthy of her position. "She maketh herself coverings of tapestry; her clothing is silk (probably purchased fresh off the merchant ships from the East) and purple," a very expensive dye which ships cruising the Mediterranean would bring to her port. I can't picture this woman begging her husband for permission to get material to make a new dress. It would have been demeaning to her and the greatness of her gentleman. Not only did she look the part of the beautiful woman she was, but she made sure those in her household had clothes of the finest colors and materials to keep them warm in wintertime. Verse 21 indicates that they were spiritually and emotionally prepared by this great woman, as well, for when sorrow and trouble came, they were not afraid.

Not only was this remarkable person buying and selling fields to satisfy her need to have special activities of her own, and making a tidy profit off the harvest, but she was at her business of making beautiful linen with the flax she had purchased. While her husband was solving weighty matters of the community, she personally buzzed off again to sell the linen and bargain with the merchants in the city about the price she should receive for the beautiful and utilitarian girdles she had made with the help of her maidens.

Women who want to be equal with men in this day of women's liberation, would emphasize, "Why didn't *she* sit in the gates and make the decisions? Why did she have to be tending to the home and limiting her talents to planting fields and making cloth? Why didn't her husband stay home and do that?"

I can't really see much difference in the two. She certainly was making some very weighty decisions which involved the town merchants (some of the wealthiest and most influential people in the country), the surrounding land owners and her own children, who would move out to make their mark upon the world. A man as wise as hers undoubtedly spent many a midnight hour talking over with his wife some of the problems he was faced with. I suspect that much of what he took to the board meetings was influenced by her wise guidance. That most certainly seems like equality to me. It seems to be a matter of where you think the spotlight should be. Personally, I would find it much more exhilarating and enlightening to be traveling about in the fresh air, as I pleased, and on my own schedule, tending to my affairs and those of my family, than sitting in a smoky, closed room, vying with others as to who would sit in the spotlight and get the glory for any moves that were made. That seems more than a bit immature to me.

Reward of Confidence

But on with our lady. Because her husband was the kind of husband God intended him to be, his wife grew in strength physically, emotionally, mentally and spiritually. We find the rest of the chapter describing the results of this desire of his to liberate his woman. She knew her husband respected what she had to say, so she had the confidence to pull upon the resources of her wise thoughts to share with him and others. In fact, "She openeth her mouth with wisdom." Her wisdom carried over into kindness. This woman didn't yell mean things at her children. She had no need to take her emotional frustrations out on them, because she was fulfilled! " . . . And in her tongue is the law of kindness."

What happened to this satisfied wife? What happened to this lady who was free to be the person God intended her to be? Joy of joys, her husband rose up, called her blessed and praised her! Papa set the scene. He let the children know what a fantastic mother they had, so they followed suit. They adored her.

The Secret

The secret to her husband's success which became her success is in verses 30 and 31. "Favor is deceitful, and beauty is vain, but a woman who feareth the Lord, she shall be praised. Give her of the fruit of her hands and let her own works praise her *in the gates*." Whoops, it looks as if she were getting in the spotlight down at the meeting hall, after all.

Let's Summarize

Proverbs 31 has pointed out to us that God's ideal woman takes in many aspects of living and behavior which is considerably broader than the average conception of it. So in summary, we see that GOD'S WOMAN:

1. RESPECTS HER HUSBAND AS THE HEAD OF HER HOUSEHOLD AND OF HER. She abides willingly by his decisions, not making life miserable for him if she doesn't get her own way. That's because he allows her to make plenty of her own decisions.

2. IS OBEDIENT TO HER HUSBAND'S WISHES. If he tells her that he likes a clean house, she will do it, not only because she respects and loves him, but because it is a challenge to her to do so. If he likes to have breakfast ready for him before he goes to work in the morning, she will have it ready. If he asks her to run to the bank for him, she will do it without impatience or irritation. She will obey him because she wants to, not because she feels she has to, for her husband has earned her respect by supplying her needs.

3. SUBMITS HERSELF TO HER HUSBAND. She is willing to go where he goes and do what he does. In physical relations, she enjoys their times together, because he used his wisdom and self-control to be a thrilling lover, and he is always considerate of her. If she has a good reason for refusing, he doesn't get angry or pout.

4. REVERENCES HER HUSBAND. She respects him and holds him in awe. Her actions show these feelings. How can she help herself? Her husband is so wise and so good, she has no choice.

5. LOVES HER HUSBAND. She works for him and with him, because he has been so ideal that her love is very, very deep. This love, in turn, causes her to bring out the best in him, encouraging him to reach full heights of achievement, because she believes in him and he knows it.

6. IS DISCREET. She is not a blabbermouth about delicate matters or things best forgotten, whether about others, or about her own family. This is helped by the fact that her husband isn't the "strong, silent type" with whom she can't communicate. She talks out her heart to him, as he does to her.

7. IS CHASTE AND VIRTUOUS. She believes in being true to her husband, and leaves the flirting to those who are still trying to catch one. She isn't afraid to be friends with other men, however, for her mature husband not only trusts her but knows that true love is not jealous. She keeps her charms for him alone, even though some magazine articles are telling her that it isn't even fashionable to admit to being married these days.

8. IS A KEEPER AT HOME. She enjoys doing the housework and rearing her children, regarding it a tremendous challenge and test of her intelligence to provide unusual meals and fun for her husband, her children and their friends. She is a fulfilled woman, even as the woman in Proverbs 31 was. She never says, "I'm just a housewife," because her husband has allowed her to develop as a person in her own right in other areas. She is much more creative and makes her home a much more fascinating place than the little flower next door who is fading and drying on the stem because her husband keeps a tight rein on her, as if she were a child.

9. IS GOOD. She reaches out to others in need. Of course she keeps her priorities straight. She is not like the young woman who adored counseling and helping others while her house was not only messy but filthy, with children running unattended.

10. IS FULL OF FAITH AND PATIENCE. She believes God and His promises, and teaches her children to do likewise. She is patient when the answers to prayers are not immediately forthcoming and gives credit to God when they are. She isn't agitating continually when her husband and children are not fitting into her scheme of things as quickly as she would like.

11. IS AGGRESSIVE. She knows what she needs to do and does it, dealing firmly but kindly with the people she comes in contact with. Her husband feels she is quite capable of handling most situations without his protective overseeing.

12. IS LIBERATED. She has interests, hobbies or even a career that makes her a tremendously fascinating woman to her husband. She is an excellent homemaker because she is bubbling with joy over the fulfillment of her dreams. She is not going "stale" over the years because of lack of stimuli. She has a husband who is mature and doesn't feel threatened by her talents and gifts. He utilizes them to his own advantage, and because she loves giving of herself she doesn't mind that.

13. IS HONORED. She is not treated as if she were one of the children. She is a thrilling, lovely woman with so much honor bestowed upon her by her husband and her children that it covers her from head to toe and makes her even more thrilling and lovely.

So there you have it, men. If your woman isn't like God's ideal, and you would like to have her be, it is imperative that you apply wisdom rather than emotion to the situation. If you have erred for years and you see it, don't let it discourage you. Tackle a few of the areas at a time, and as they start improving, reach out for others! If you are determined and clever, in time you will be successful.

The majority of Christian women are not straining hard at the bit as yet, generally speaking. While the woman of the world is screaming "suppression" the Christian woman is content, by and large, to sacrifice her dreams and abilities to keep her husband happy, and as the years go by, is willing to forget she ever had them. She tells herself, "It must have been the Lord's will," and her husband is smugly satisfied that she is all she ever wanted to be. But more and more, Christian women are muttering out of the corner of their mouths. They are feeling frustrated. Blame the world, if you wish. But the problem is a real one, and one you may have to deal with if you aren't willing to be the kind of husband God wants you to be.

●

P.S. to the ideal wife to be: impossible, you may be saying! No woman could be that good! Yes, a woman can. And you can. Want to be truly happy and filled to overflowing with joy and peace? Then this is your answer. Look to the Source of Power from above, and it will be even easier. It's time to get going!

13

The Ideal Husband

So what is an ideal husband? Can we fit him into a neat little mold and say, "Be this way," or "Be that way?" No. Every husband is a unique individual who is "fearfully and wonderfully made," as King David noted in the Psalms.

Scriptural Guidelines

Your relationship with your wife will be different from any other husband-wife relationship in the world! But there are certain guidelines laid out by God for a man. They are written in man's conscience if he heeds it. They are also written in the Bible. Summarizing what we have found thus far and adding to it what we have not yet explored, we see that the ideal husband:

1. IS WILLING TO SPEND TIME using his marvelous mentality to dwell with his wife in KNOWLEDGE. He figures out why she is like she is and sets about to help her overcome her weaknesses by applying his knowledge of her basic nature, and proceeding accordingly.

2. IS WILLING TO SUPPLY HER NEEDS, even though his practical soul tells him it is nonsense. This fantastic mate supplies the WORDS and the ACTIONS that spell ROMANCE to his wife. He treats her like the lovely little flower she is, careful not to crush her with his masculine insensitivity.

3. REALIZES THAT HER SEXUAL RESPONSE will be in direct proportion to his determination to supply her emotional needs. Here is a man who becomes a lover that would make Solomon envious. His wife enjoys their physical union as much as he does.

4. IS WILLING TO SACRIFICE HIS OWN COMFORT in order to lovingly help his wife keep a good home. This Dream Of All Women gets bigger in stature and greatness as he bends to help, guide and lead. ". . . Speaking the truth in love," he *organizes* and *works.* He makes chores around home a fun thing for his wife, the children and himself.

5. REALIZES THAT AS A MAN, IT IS TIME TO PUT AWAY CHILDISH THINGS. He becomes mature in his thinking.

6. TREATS ALL WOMEN WITH GENTLENESS AND RESPECT. As a consequence, many women mentally fall in line behind him. He is wise enough

to realize, however, that their adoration is because they are being starved emotionally and not because he is some Greek Adonis. He is also wise enough to realize that he can destroy his wife if he doesn't keep her as the center of his love and attention and all other relationships secondary to her.

7. RECOGNIZES THAT HE IS INCOMPLETE if he neglects the spiritual part of his life. He finds out that a man who rises from his knees after spending time in a prayer of repentence to Almighty God is taller and mightier than the greatest of earthly kings who have not done likewise.

8. PROVIDES FOR HIS FAMILY. Instinctively he knows it is shameful and unmanly for a man not to take care of his family's needs financially, emotionally, spiritually and physically. Indeed, the Bible backs him up for it says, "But if any provide not for his own, and specially for those of his own house, he hath denied the faith, and is worse than an infidel." That includes life insurance—a must. It means a properly-drawn will so his children will have a home and income if he and his wife pass on to better things.

God doesn't draw the line there. He's got more goodies for you to chew on. So, on to one that will need a little expanding. The ideal husband . . .

9. IS HEAD OF THE WIFE! We sent out a survey questionnaire to people whom we were reasonably sure were Christians who attended church regularly and who believed in the Bible as the inspired Word of God. The results of the survey, which was anonymous, presented a startling contrast to the surveys of the public in general. Here were marriages that were stable. Their problems were generally minor and nothing they felt they couldn't

handle. The wives were, on a whole, happier than their general public counterparts, for the husbands were more inclined to supply their needs. However, it was clear, by the woman's surveys, that they felt their husbands needed to do more of all the right things they were doing. The husbands in this group were helped considerably by the fact that their wives wanted to obey God and to be the women they were instructed to be in the Scriptures. Both were willing to make allowances. Even though these Christian men were not ideal by a long shot (nor were their women), there was much to be learned from them. Both sexes agreed that the husband should be the head of the wife according to Ephesians 5:23: "For the husband is the head of the wife, even as Christ is the head of the church. . . ."

When asked what they felt being "head of the wife" meant, the usual answer was, "When there is disagreement on a matter and a stalemate results, the man is to make the decision." Most of them rejected a "chain of command" type of relationship which tends to put Papa up as the totalitarian leader.

There was a time when George decided he wasn't getting enough respect as head of our family. He had read an article by another man and came home determined to change things. I noticed it immediately, for he would bark an order and when I didn't jump up and ask why on the way down, he would say with firm finality, "I'm the head of this house and when I say something I want it done NOW."

The children looked at him as if they secretly wondered if he had flipped. This went on for several days. This was not the man who had changed me so totally, who recognized me as a person and not a servant. So finally, when we were alone, I said, "Honey, you've changed. You aren't the same person you used to be. I just don't think I want to live the rest of my life with an irritable, over-bearing, pushy husband who has forgotten I am a mature woman and a partner and treats me like a child." I was honest with my feelings, telling him frankly what I thought. Since he is a mature man, and unlike those who were advising him wrongly, he quickly saw how foolish he was behaving and went back to being the one who rules lovingly, compellingly and with wisdom.

The Truly Wise Man

"Who is a wise man . . . among you? Let him show out of a good conversation his works with meekness of wisdom. But if ye have bitter envying and strife in your hearts, glory not, and lie not against the truth. This wisdom descendeth not from above, but is earthly, sensual, devilish. But the wisdom that is from above is first pure, then peaceable, gentle, and easy to be entreated, full of mercy and good fruits, without partiality, and without hypocrisy."

In the "good old days" women often grew old before their time or died young. The husband and wife weren't always friends. They tended more toward a father-daughter or master-servant type of relationship. Good for selfish, bullheaded Pop perhaps, but not so good for poor Mom. At least he felt it kept him in his proper place as head of the family. And there is a movement today, urging families to get back to this type of government. However, as you can see by the Scriptures at which we have already looked, the Bible does not support that type of approach. God has His own ideas, despite what man or woman thinks.

But that isn't all. The ideal husband. . .

10. GIVES HONOR UNTO HIS WIFE. I'll never forget the day I met Billy Graham in a receiving line. He was quietly reserved but gracious. His eyes were startling in their unusual color and his strength was that of a man who walks very close

to his God. If it had been my good fortune to host this gentleman, I would have treated him with great honor.

Is there someone you would give honor to if you had the opportunity? A visitor is in a vulnerable position. He is as welcome or unwelcome as the host allows.

A Celebrity in the House?

Let's say the Queen of England came to stay overnight in your home. Would you tell her off loud and clear if she didn't get her bed made in the morning? Would you ignore her in the evening, burying your head in the newspaper? Would you tell her she was a big baby if she started protesting about the kind of treatment you were giving her? If she prepared some of her favorite food so you could taste a queen's menu, would you gobble it down without a word of thanks or appreciation? Of course not. The idea is ludicrous. (Even the picture of the Queen entering a "common" person's home and cooking a dinner is ludicrous.) You would treat *any* such personage with as much honor as you could muster, wouldn't you?

Guess what? Your wife is just such a personage. The Bible says you are to give *honor* to your wife!

"What?" gasps the head of the wife. "You've got to be out of your mind! I'm to give my wife the kind of treatment I would give a celebrity?" I didn't say it. God did. Honor is honor, regardless of how you spell it. But if that shakes you up a little, hang on tight. There's more coming. The entire verse referring to honoring your wife reads like this:

"In like manner, ye husbands, dwell with them according to knowledge, giving honor unto the wife, as unto the weaker vessel, and as being heirs together of the grace of life, that your prayers be not hindered" (1 Peter 3:7).

God says it is so important for you to live with

your wife according to knowledge (not ego or emotion) and that you give honor to her, that He makes it clear if you DON'T, your prayers will not be of much use. Isn't that what the last of that verse says—". . . that your prayers be not hindered"? Maybe you have wondered why your prayers are ineffectual a good portion of the time. Maybe you have wished you could see POWER in your life and abundant answers to your petitions.

Whew, it does seem that this husband-wife business might be more important than we thought! Never mind that you are better to your wife than "Sloppy Sam" or Volcano Victor. God isn't in the business of comparisons. He compares you with only one person —His Son. How do you stack up?

Let's go on to explore deeply the ideal husband who . . .

11. LOVES HIS WIFE EVEN AS CHRIST LOVED THE CHURCH. "So ought men to love their wives as their own bodies. He that loveth his wife loveth himself. For no man ever yet hated his own flesh, but nourisheth and cherisheth it, even as the Lord the church" (Ephesians 5:28, 29).

The Bible is a story of LOVE. God's love. And God feels that love—sincere deep love—is very, very important. The great love chapter of the Bible is 1 Corinthians 13. Let's see how Mr. Ideal Husband fits into that chapter.

"Love suffereth long and is kind," we read. Here's a man that puts up with all kinds of injustice from his family and yet continues to be kind to them, not cruel. Of course he realizes that he is not being kind if he lets them get away with disobedience and disrespect. He firmly but kindly deals with it.

He envies neither his wife nor his children as he sees them "shine" in certain areas of their lives. In fact, in verse 4, we are told that a man who loves in the right way, doesn't spend his time telling the world how great he is or even working overtime to be sure he takes care of NUMBER ONE. Here's a man who doesn't participate in activities that bring shame to his family or himself. In verse 6 we're told he "rejoiceth not in iniquity," even if the fellows he'd like to impress are the ones indulging in forbidden fruit. That sort of thing brings a big stomachache. He would be apt to choose different friends in the long run anyway; friends who believe in decency.

Back to verse 5. Here's a giant among men who doesn't get riled easily. He isn't quick to jump to conclusions concerning something his children do, or his wife. He listens carefully before drawing his conclusions. He is very patient, for (verse 7) he "beareth all things, believeth all things, hopeth all things, endureth all things." He doesn't run off and leave his wife when she begins to lose her former beauty. Instead he sees a new, deeper and lovelier beauty in her for his love "never faileth."

What a Man!

One of the finest examples of a man understanding what love is, was presented by a psychologist at a Family Conference I was privileged to attend. Evidently he and his wife had come to the conclusion that they needed a hi-fi. The only problem was, they couldn't decide which one. One of them wanted a very expensive set and the other, a very inexpensive set. Since they couldn't come to an agreement both were adamant on which would be the proper choice. Thus they deferred to the fact that as head of the house, the husband would have to break the stalemate and make the decision. He said he faced his responsibility soberly. Scripture commanded him to honor his wife and love her as his own body. Even the golden rule crept into his thoughts. He was to do unto others as he would have them do unto him. After some contemplation, and I'm sure, a bit of wrestling with temptation, he made his decision, which he did not reveal to his audience. To this day, he keeps this secret. But no doubt was left in the minds of his listeners as to what a spiritually mature man *should* decide in a case like that.

I can look back time and again in my own married life when my husband has made the decision to obey Christ rather than self, putting my desires above his own. At times it has astounded me and I have felt that I would do anything within my power to express my gratitude to him.

There is even more to this love-your-wife business. Most men would run to the rescue of their wives if they were being threatened physically in some way. And most men would be quick to defend their wives should someone insult them or speak disparagingly about them. In fact, I would like to believe that most would go to their *death* to save their wives, although no one can predetermine a thing like *that!* Certainly one of the greatest men of God there ever was, Abraham, failed that test.

His wife, beautiful even in her old age, was given to a king by her frightened husband to become a member of the king's harem. This weak-kneed hubby instructed his wife to say that she was his sister, not his wife. Well, she was his half sister in reality, and I suppose he felt a little white lie wasn't all that bad. What the Pharoah didn't know wouldn't hurt him, would it?

Why did Abraham do this? To save his own neck, that's why! Happily enough for Sarai, the Pharoah found out the truth, released her and gave Abe the dressing down of his life.

Life is very precious, and all of us would think twice about giving it up willingly. But nevertheless, let us assume that you would do so if your wife's life were at stake. That sort of action is *noble* and *manly*. Besides, you were cut out for that sort of thing, what with your muscles and all. As Christ died for the church, then, you would die for your wife, right?

But there is another way that Christ gave Himself for the church (you and me) and that way might not seem so noble and manly to you, especially if it means applying it to your own case. Look at this mind-blower:

"Let this mind be in you, which was also in Christ Jesus who, being in the form of God, thought it not robbery to be equal with God, but made himself of no reputation and took upon him the form of a servant, and was made in the likeness of men; and being found in fashion as a man, he humbled himself. . . ."

Did I see right? Christ, who came from the heavens where He ruled the universe, became like a servant?

Now, that's giving. That's LOVE.

After Jesus washed the disciples feet, he said, "If I, then, your Lord and Master, have washed your feet, ye also ought to wash one another's feet. For I have given you an example, that ye should do as I have done to you."

It wasn't the feet that was the important thing. Jesus wanted his disciples to serve one another.

If you are a Christian, what is the first thing you do when you get into trouble that seems beyond human help? Of course. You call upon the Lord. You expect Him not only to listen, but to heed what you are requesting. You expect Him to answer. He is at your beck and call. He doesn't let you down. He hears and He hastens to aid you. He supplies your needs and probably most of your wants and desires. He will say no to some of your requests in order to do what is best for you. He is truly KING, but He is truly SERVANT, serving us and tenderly caring for us.

"Husbands, love your wives, even as Christ also loved the church" for He "took upon him the form of a servant . . . and humbled himself."

There it is. Once again, I didn't say it. God did.

Spoil Her?

"Won't that make a very selfish wife," you may ask? "Spoil a woman like that and she'll take advantage of you." Very few would, for it is woman's nature to give more than she takes. Her estimation of a husband who treats *her* as Christ treats *him* shoots up like a geyser. If this type of honor and loving becomes the rule rather than the exception, her admiration will know no bounds and she will become almost putty in her husband's hands. How wonderful to "spoil" her a little in order to obey God and reap the rewards of her reverence for you.

As we said before, most of the women in the liberation movement have no idea that God understood their needs and ordered men to supply them long ago, and that had men understood and heeded, they would be satisfied. All they know is that something is wrong, and since men won't correct it, they will. I sympathize with the need that is crying out from their hearts, but they are looking in the wrong direction for the answer.

In our survey we asked the following question:

"Do you feel you treat your wife as Christ treated the church? If yes, in which of the following ways:

_____I make all decisions for her welfare rather than mine.

_____I allow her to use her abilities and talents to their fullest.

_____I show patience in all situations.

_____I try to be a servant to her, attending to her needs.

_____I show her kindness.

_____I allow her to make many decisions.

_____I treat her as a partner, not my servant.

_____I forgive her when she transgresses.

_____I try to guide her when she needs it in making decisions.

_____She can talk with me about anything without my getting angry.

Most husbands answering the questionnaire saw themselves as almost the perfect husband, even though the wives' matching surveys didn't reveal quite the same thing. And on both surveys, we saw very few checks in front of "I try to be a servant to her, attending to her needs." That one was too much for the large majority of the men to take.

So our last point on what the ideal husband should be is ...

12. HE BECOMES AS A SERVANT TO HIS WIFE,
tending to her requests and needs even as Christ tends to his.

Don't go away, yet. That pill was a hard one to swallow, I know. Good things often come that way. It is *easy* to go the wrong way. But ". . . with God, nothing shall be impossible."

Marvelous men, you are so strong. Lend that strength to the weak. You are so intelligent. Handle your wives with knowledge. You are appointed. God put much responsibility in your hands. He wouldn't have done so if he had felt you were not equipped to handle it. I wouldn't have believed it possible for a man if I hadn't experienced it from my own husband. Since then, I have seen it in others as well.

> He drew a circle that shut me out—
> Heretic, rebel, a thing to flout.
> But Love and I had the wit to win
> We drew a circle that took him in.
> Edwin Markham, *Familiar Quotations*

Substitute "she" for "he" in that poem and think of your wife. She is waiting to be transformed into a princess even if she isn't aware of it yet. Brains or brawn. Willing service or reluctance. Obedience or scorn. Patience and loving determination or refusal to try. The decision is up to you.

*

P.S. Dear Lady, a good man nowadays is hard to find, they say. One internationally-known actress of great beauty states that a woman who wears the pants in her family will live to see her husband's mistress wearing mink and diamonds. You were meant to be his helper, not his competition. But you can encourage him to get into the Scriptures and to follow them. And you can be the greatest influence in his life if you do so yourself. Your husband is worth all your effort! As he begins to become a BETTER MAN, I hope you will fervently be about the business of being a BETTER WIFE.

Bibliography

The Amplified New Testament. Grand Rapids, Michigan, Zondervan Publishing House, 1958.

The Authorized King James Version of the Holy Bible, Edited by Rev. C. I. Scofield, D.D. (Old and New Testaments), 1969.

Bartlett, John. *Familiar Quotations.* Garden City, New York, Garden City Publishing Co., Inc., 1945.

The Best Loved Poems of the American People. Poems selected by Hazel Felleman, Garden City, New York, Doubleday and Company, Inc., 1936.

LaHaye, Tim. *How To Be Happy Though Married.* Wheaton, Illinois, Tyndale House Publishers, 1970.

LaHaye, Tim. *Spirit Controlled Temperament.* Wheaton, Illinois, Tyndale House Publishers, 1973.

Lewin, S. A., M.D., and Gilmore, John, Ph.D. *Sex Without Fear.* New York, Medical Research Press, 1972.

The Marriage Affair, Edited by J. Allen Petersen. Wheaton, Illinois, Tyndale House Publishers, 1971.

McMillen, S. I., M.D. *None of These Diseases.* Westwood, New Jersey, Fleming H. Revell Company (Spire Books), 1968.

Miles, Herbert J., Ph.D. *Sexual Happiness in Marriage.* Grand Rapids, Michigan, Zondervan Publishing House, 1974.

Nittler, Alan H., M.D. *A New Breed of Doctor.* New York, Pyramid Books, 1974.

One Hundred and One Famous Poems. An Anthology compiled by Roy J. Cook, Chicago, Illinois, The Reilly & Lee Co. Publishers, 1958.

Strauss, Richard L. *Marriage Is For Love*. Wheaton, Illinois, Tyndale House Publishers, 1973.

"Women's Lib in Russia: The Myth and the Reality," *U.S. News & World Report*, 16 November 1970, page 75.

Scripture References

All references are from the King James Version of the Holy Bible unless otherwise indicated.

NOTES

1. "Men's Survey and Women's Survey," by Margie Ministries, 1974. A survey questionnaire, covering many aspects of the marriage relationship, was sent to and answered anonymously by married, divorced and widowed men and women of various ages and occupations. The majority of the participants were church related.
2. *Sex Habits of European Women vs. American Women* by Herbert C. Rosenthal, Pageant.
3. All medical information in this chapter was derived from Alan H. Nittler, M.D., author of *A New Breed of Doctor* (see Bibliography).
4. Lawrence J. Crabb, Jr., Ph.D. "A Biblical Guide to Sex in Marriage." *Christian Life,* February, 1973, p. 40.
5. "Secret Hideout," heard on Family Stations, Inc., and on affiliated stations.
6. Bruce Larson, "Are You Fun to Live With?" *Today,* Harvest Publications, Evanston, Illinois.